Also by Peter Manseau

Killing the Buddha
<small>(WITH JEFF SHARLET)</small>

Vows

Songs for the Butcher's Daughter

RAG AND BONE

RAG AND BONE

A Journey Among the World's Holy Dead

PETER MANSEAU

A HOLT PAPERBACK
HENRY HOLT AND COMPANY   NEW YORK

Holt Paperbacks
Henry Holt and Company, LLC
Publishers since 1866
175 Fifth Avenue
New York, New York 10010
www.henryholt.com

Distributed in Canada by H. B. Fenn and Company Ltd.

Images that appear on the opening pages of chapters 1, 2, 4, 5, 7 & 8 are courtesy of the National Library of Medicine.

Images that appear on the opening pages of chapters 3 & 6 are courtesy of the author's collection.

Library of Congress Cataloging-in-Publication Data

Manseau, Peter.
   Rag and bone: a journey among the world's holy dead / Peter Manseau.—1st ed.
      p. cm.
   ISBN: 978-0-8050-9147-2
   1. Relics.   I. Title.

BL619.R44M36 2009
203'.7—dc22   2008039465

Henry Holt books are available for special promotions and premiums.
For details contact: Director, Special Markets.

Originally published in hardcover in 2009 by Henry Holt and Company

First Holt Paperbacks Edition 2010

Designed by Meryl Sussman Levavi

Printed in the United States of America

10 9 8 7 6 5 4 3 2 1

IF ANYTHING IS SACRED,

THE HUMAN BODY IS SACRED.

—WALT WHITMAN

CONTENTS

RAG AND BONE

IN THE BEGINNING
WAS THE TONGUE

THIS IS A BOOK ABOUT DISMEMBERED TOES, SPLINTERS OF shinbone, stolen bits of hair, burned remnants of an anonymous rib cage, and other odds and ends of human remains, but it is not a book about death. Around every one of the macabre artifacts that, for a variety of reasons, have come to be venerated as religious relics, circles an endless orbit of believers and skeptics, bureaucrats and clergy, fathers and mothers and children, pilgrims, beggars, con artists, and just plain curious souls. This is a book about life.

Before I saw my first relic, about ten years ago, I stood for what seemed like hours in a line of tourists wrapped around the altar of an Italian basilica, under a tableau of the stations of the cross carved in wood. Each of the stations' fourteen squares depicted a scene from the crucifixion as large and menacing as a horror movie poster, but no one paid them much attention. Everyone was too busy checking their watches, folding pages in their Umbria guidebooks, laughing and grumbling and planning in a dozen languages.

Directly in front of me, a young mother with dyed black hair and a matching biker jacket watched her toddling son clap his palms on the polished floor and then warned him in German—"*Nicht anfassen!*" *Don't touch that!*—each time he put his hands on something that seemed dirty or fragile. The boy had blond hair and spitty wet fingers and was eyeing a piece of dried gum stuck to one of the basilica's marble columns. Both column and gum seemed to have been there for an eternity, but when the boy pinched the gray wad his mother hissed—"*Horst! Nein!*"—as if its removal would bring the whole place tumbling down.

The line shuffled forward and little Horst fell in behind his parents, tucking his face into the back of his father's knees. Latching on with one hand to a fold of green denim, inserting his other hand in his mouth for safekeeping, he let his feet drag on the ground to show how bored he was with all of this. He seemed to be about three, and I wondered if his parents had tried to explain why they had brought him to this dark church in the middle of a lovely autumn day. Had he understood what he was waiting for, he might have appeared more excited.

At the end of this line, which stretched from the entrance fifty yards behind us to a point farther ahead than we could see, there was said to be a very special tongue. A human tongue from a human head. A tongue that was believed to have the power to give speech to the dumb and eloquence to the tongue-tied. A tongue so potent—legend and guidebooks proclaim—that it was found whole, pink, and healthy after the body it had spoken for had gone to dust.

It was not just any tongue, but *La lingua del Santo,* "The Tongue of the Saint." In the ancient city of Padua, two hundred miles or so north of Rome, "the saint" refers always and only to Saint Anthony, whose basilica this was. Born at the end of the twelfth century in Portugal but embraced most fervently by Italian Catholics, Saint Anthony is the patron saint of lost objects. All of us, a thousand tourists on any given day, were there to see what was left of him.

I was standing on my tiptoes, craning my neck over the crowd to have a look at the end of the line, when someone made a *pssst* noise and others clucked in agreement, raising and pointing their chins in a gesture meant to urge me on. I turned to see that the line had moved forward. There was now ten feet of empty floor between the German family and me. I put my hand in the air as apology to the waiting throng and half-jogged to close the gap.

When I got there, Horst was stretched out on the floor. His mother glanced back and then hoisted him up by his belt, apologizing with her eyes.

The pilgrims lurched forward, around a bend now, and I followed the Germans into a narrow passage behind the altar.

Five yards ahead, the line changed from relative order to a small-scale mob. Some stopped and turned to the left to take a long look while others forced their way through the traffic of bodies, impatient to move on now that the waiting was done. I couldn't yet see what was causing the commotion, but it was impossible to miss the fireworks of camera flashes blinking off the walls, despite the repeated warnings we'd all received against turning this holy place into a photo shoot.

At least our crowd wanted only pictures. Back in the heyday of Christian relic veneration—roughly the eleventh century through the sixteenth, when the Protestant Reformation brought the boom times of relics to an end—religious authorities had to keep constant guard over the sacred remains they displayed. A story is told of an English bishop who, while on pilgrimage in France, toured a monastery that had a shrine containing the full skeleton of Mary Magdalene. Impressing the monks with his piety, the bishop stooped to put his lips on the holy lady's hand. No one noticed that, by the end of his kiss, he had bitten off a piece of her finger. He held it in his mouth for the rest of the monastery tour, then returned to England to build a shrine of his own.

So it's no surprise the basilica guards were content to let the tongue photos slide. Not that they could have done much about it. The number and speed of the flashes in the passageway suggested that the crowd of Australians, Germans, Koreans, and at least half a dozen other nationalities was intent on spending its time in Padua as paparazzi of the holy dead.

In the middle of the hubbub, a family of four had dropped to their knees in front of the entrance to a small chapel, which I could now see was to blame for the gridlock.

"*La Cappella delle Reliquie,*" an Italian whispered behind me. From others in line I heard it identified in French and Spanish as *La Chapelle des Reliques* and *La Capilla de las Reliquias,* "The Chapel of the Relics," though a sign in English identified it with less poetry as "The Treasury." It contained Saint Anthony's tongue, jawbone, and a small piece of cartilage believed to be part of his larynx.

The kneeling family had been mostly silent through the forty minutes I'd been in line, so I couldn't guess their nationality, but their manner and dress suggested they were some variety of Europeans. When they rose, they crossed themselves with the absentminded ease of Crusaders' distant kin. Wherever they were from in what remains of Christendom, kneeling before pieces of a saint was a part of them, as it had been for generations beyond memory, a tradition unchanged for a thousand years.

The Germans fought their way through the throng, and I followed close behind, moving easily through the wake created by the stroller the father pushed before him. When the mother reached the reliquary, her mouth dropped open. She called out to her son, "*Horst! Guch mal! Eine Zunge!*"

But Horst didn't seem to hear her. He turned and ran into the crowd, disappearing among the tourists' legs as their cameras flashed like strobe lights. When his mother raced to catch him, it was finally my turn to approach the tongue.

Reaching the pedestal on which it stood, I was surprised to see that the reliquary looked like nothing so much as a model lighthouse: a tall, thin column supporting a crystal cylinder—though in this case the cylinder contained not a lantern but a cone-shaped chunk of human flesh, a tiny scrap of body behind glass.

As the story goes, at the time of its discovery in the saint's tomb eight hundred years before, the tongue had been so moist and plump it looked ready to deliver a sermon all on its own. Now, the ornamentation of the gold around it seemed more appropriate for the Hope diamond than for the chewed piece of licorice the tongue had come to resemble. The pedestal was spotted with fingerprints, and more than a few pilgrims went so far as to stand on their toes to plant kisses directly on the marble around the reliquary's base. Centuries of such contact had added a greasy bit of color to the gray stone, a soft pink mix of lipstick, finger oil, and spit, evidence that as many people as there were smudges had stood on this spot and tried to make contact with *Il Santo* and, through him, with God.

I put my fingers to my mouth and then as close to the relic as I could reach. The stone was cold to the touch but slightly slick, like a sweating beer bottle on a summer day.

On the way out, I saw little lost Horst out of the corner of my eye. He had wandered alone into the corner of the chapel and now stood puzzling over what all the fuss was about. One hand down his pants, the other up his nose, he looked on the traffic jam of adults crowding the holy tongue like he was the only one with his priorities straight.

＊

THOUGH IT HAS now been a decade since I saw Saint Anthony's tongue, the weirdness of waiting in line with the citizens of the world to view an extravagantly displayed piece of human flesh has never left me. I had been raised Catholic and so I was familiar with the idea of relics but, having never before traveled to Europe, that was the first time I had seen one that looked like anything other than a bug under glass. Outside Catholic circles, it is a little-known fact that every Roman Catholic church has a relic. In the United States, they are usually hidden discreetly within the altar at the front of the church. These relics are rarely viewed, however, and when they are, on feast days, or at shrines built specifically for that purpose, they more closely resemble a gnat or a thread or a pebble than anything holy. For the majority of relics in the Americas, holiness comes only through association: often they really are just threads or pebbles, tiny scraps of clothing or objects believed to have once made physical contact with a saint.

Throughout my Catholic youth it had been easy to ignore relics. Standing before Saint Anthony was the first time I had looked on a religious artifact and realized that the object I was looking at was not just a *what* but a *who*. The equal parts shock and fascination this realization inspired were experienced anew with each relic I saw in the years that followed: the head of Saint Catherine, a finger of John the Baptist, a pebble of enamel chipped from the Buddha's tooth. I've spent the better part of the past decade thinking and writing about the fringes of religion, and even as other oddities of spiritual practice become old hat, this particular strangeness continues to fascinate me. I am moved not only by the miraculous powers many relics are said to have, nor merely by questions of their authenticity, but also simply by the fact of them, the fleshy actuality of what they are.

What they are, of course, are remnants of saints, prophets, and sages: the keepsakes and castoffs of consecrated women and men, and most of all their bodies. The word itself—at the root, the Latin *reliquus*—refers to "something left over or kept behind." Considered this way, relics are also one of the very few things that truly connect the religions of the world. Every religion is a banquet of holy lives; these are the leftovers. Another possible translation of *reliquus* sums up the objects' meaning and power succinctly: relics are simply "what remains."

Relics have been revered by believers all over the world because all over the world the people who believers believe in die. This may be a tautology, but it's also true: in any belief system in which humans play a role (all of them, that is), the death of those who speak of life beyond death is bound to become a problem. Some die peacefully of natural causes (such as the Buddha, who delivered so many different sets of last words his followers might have wondered if he would ever really leave), some die of disease (the battle-hardened Muhammad is thought to have been finally done in by malaria), some are victims of violence (name any early

Christian martyr), and others are believed to have simply been taken up to heaven (the Virgin Mary, for one, as well as a variety of Hindu sages). What all these different religious figures have in common is worship focused on, and the occasional battle over, their physical remains. The breastbone of the Buddha, the breast milk of the Virgin, the tooth of the Prophet, the uncut hair of Hindu ascetics believed to have passed on to another realm: all have been at the center of religious conviction and conflict.

And relics have been there, more or less, since the beginning. Though they have become embarrassing reminders of the dark ages of faith to many progressive believers, the fact is that no religion, no matter how forward thinking its members consider themselves today, has been untouched by some sort of relic veneration in its past. Every religious tradition that has survived the centuries has done so through a near-constant expansion into new territory, finding new adherents wherever it roamed. To do so successfully, a new faith required some kind of calling card, a portable form of sanctity for its far-flung outposts to rally around. In the cases of Christianity, Islam, and Buddhism especially, these calling cards—not quite seeds of community but certainly fertilizer—were relics. Even traditions such as Judaism and Hinduism, which have shunned prolonged handling of the dead, have had relics of a sort: priceless mementos of the earliest or most trying days of the faith, reminders that even traditions that seem to have always existed were, once upon a time, as awkward and fragile as newborns.

To look on a relic is to see an artifact of this creation.

Even if an object is not genuinely what believers profess it to be—such as Chaucer's feather of the angel Gabriel—it becomes the locus of belief for centuries. And it is in this belief that faith is made. For the faithful, to pray to a relic displayed in its reliquary—even to a blackened and shriveled tongue—is like shining sunlight through a magnifying glass. A relic concentrates the beliefs surrounding it until they can be seen; it is a faith so intense it has, at times, set the world on fire.

✳

THIS IS NOT just ancient history. When Cardinal Joseph Ratzinger became Pope Benedict XVI in the spring of 2005, one of his first acts of private devotion as pope was to close himself in his Vatican apartment with the heart of the patron saint of priests, Saint Jean-Baptiste-Marie Vianney, who was famous in life for being able to "read the hearts" of those who came to him to confess their sins. Saint Jean-Baptiste reportedly heard confessions eighteen hours a day during the last year of his life. Usually kept in a shrine in France, his heart had been brought to Rome in honor of the dying Pope John Paul II, and as a symbol that the new pope should likewise strive to be a reader of the hearts of the faithful.

A few years before, the heart of a recently deceased Tibetan lama is believed to have selected the lama's own successor. As a gathering of monks was ritually preparing the lama's body for cremation, the heart is said to have jumped off the altar. It landed on the floor, squished here and there as the monks tried to grab it and continue their ceremony, and finally somehow found its way out the door and into the crowd awaiting the cremation. By the time the heart came to a stop, it was at the feet of a ten-year-old boy. After some deliberation as to what this might mean, the monks declared that the dead lama's reincarnation had been found. Today the boy, now in his early twenties, is a young but much respected Buddhist teacher.

Did the dead heart really jump? I tend to think not. But I also wonder if the truth of such a story matters, or rather *how* it matters. While questions of relics' origins and provenance fascinate me, to see a finger believed to be that of John the Baptist is to see an object that people have come to kneel before and pray to for centuries. I am as interested in the stories it has inspired as in the story of the object itself. Indeed, if it is not actually John the Baptist's finger, it is potentially all the more interesting. I can still see that particular relic in my mind's eye: discolored and bent but with a well-manicured nail; thanks to the shriveling of years it is almost child-sized—think of the tiny digit Horst slid up his nose—but nonetheless it is clearly a human finger. Which raises the question: if not the prophet John's, then whose?

The stories told about relics—both their origins and their effects—immediately become the stuff of legend, and yet because they are fully grounded in the body, they are also the stuff of real life. They serve at once as storyteller, observer, object, history, myth, and, of course, all that remains of someone who, way back when, was perhaps mistaken for a saint.

And the stories of relics are not just about how particular traditions learn from their past; they are also about how they define themselves within, and often against, the rest of the world.

In the sixteenth century, John Calvin and his cohorts in the second generation of the Protestant Reformation delivered their most scornful attacks against the papacy by hitting where many Roman Catholics considered below the belt, with a few quick and cutting jabs at relics. Of the Virgin Mary's breast milk, Calvin wrote, "It cannot be necessary to enumerate all the places where it is shown. Indeed, the task would be endless, for there is no town, however small, no monastery or nunnery, however insignificant, which does not possess it, some in less, and others in greater quantities." He further commented that all questions of preservation for fifteen hundred years aside, it was physically impossible for so much milk to have ever been in existence. "Had Mary been a cow all her life," he concluded, "she could not have produced such a quantity."

In the decades of unrest that followed, relics became a wedge that drove the church even further apart. Anti-Catholic tracts such as *The Pope's Warehouse, or The Inventory of the Whore of Rome* (published and widely read in London in 1679) followed Calvin's lead and elaborated his implication: that, as far as they were concerned, the greed of Rome was so boundless it would hoard even the corpses of its most beloved. Not that the Calvinists remained without sin. In 1572, they captured nineteen Catholic priests in the Dutch coastal town of Gorkum. Refusing to renounce practices such as the veneration of relics, the priests were hanged from the rafters of a turf shed. It was a bit of poetic justice, if cold comfort to the dead men, that the murder scene became a Catholic pilgrimage destination and the bodies of the "Martyrs of Gorkum" were spirited away to be enshrined in a church in Brussels.

Such was the way the drama of relics dominated and directed the times. The Reformation was in many ways a defining event for Western civilization; it triggered domino effects of schisms within schisms that eventually divided Europe and sent splinter groups looking for new lands—including the one colonized by the people we now call the Pilgrims. Look below the surface of the conflicts that followed the Reformation and you can find relics buried deep down within these histories, like bits of shrapnel that remain even after the wounds have healed.

The same can be said of an intrareligious rift that is shaping the world today. In the news every night we hear of the difficulty of finding peace in the Middle East and Central Asia, regions both at war with outside forces and bitterly divided between Shia and Sunni Muslims. Broadly speaking, the Shiites revere relics; the Sunnis despise them. In Saudi Arabia, the Wahhabi government of fundamentalist Sunnis has bulldozed relic-containing mosques and shrines they see as examples of idolatry. At another spot in the Muslim world, when the Taliban first attempted to take control of Afghanistan in 1996, they knew where to begin. The Taliban leader Mullah Omar demanded to be let into a shrine containing relics of the Prophet Muhammad: hair from his beard and a cloak he is said to have worn. Seizing the cloak, Mullah Omar went to the roof of the shrine and slid his hands into the sleeves, holding the garment before him for everyone to see. To the crowd watching, it looked like he had gone into the relic chamber and come out transformed into the Prophet himself.

As in the Christian world five centuries before, the power of relics, whether unleashed through their destruction or their glorification, is today being used in the Muslim world to send a message about worldly and otherworldly control. Seen this way, the "clash of civilizations" in which our cultures are sometimes said to be engaged includes the clatter of some very old bones.

To look upon the world's religious differences through the lens of relics sheds light on why such differences are often so difficult to understand. Relics are as complicated and varied as the human beings they once were. Whether a tooth, a heart, a whisker, or a calcified tear, these items have exerted a remarkable and complicated influence in the world for such tiny, often frankly repulsive, things. It is no surprise that we sometimes recognize the stories told about relics as having to do with matters of life or death: they are always about both.

✳

NOT TOO LONG ago, I was reminded of my visit with Saint Anthony when I stood looking at another body through glass. I was standing not in a church but in a medical examination room. As I waited to see the figure, there was no crowd to fight—just the doctor, my wife, and me.

A blurry white blob is all we saw. The doctor typed on the keyboard below the monitor and an arrow appeared near the blob's center. He moved his finger across a small touch pad and directed the arrow to the blob's rounded end.

"Head," he said. The arrow slid down the blob's perimeter. "Arms . . . legs . . ."

I squinted and moved closer to the image. I had assumed that at this first glimpse of our first child I would be overwhelmed by the fetus's wholeness, the primordial personhood visible on the screen. Instead, I was struck by the assemblage of parts, present and pending, in various states of completeness. In a few weeks I would get used to calling this assemblage *she*, a daughter.

The doctor moved the sensor slightly, and we watched as the baby rolled, as if turning to face us, though, of course, she could not see anything at all. When our view of her changed, so, it seemed, did her substance; with our new perspective, the tiny twigs that were becoming her bones became visible, spine and ribs and skull.

Later, when I thought back on this first image of my daughter through the dark glass, I was as surprised as anyone would have been that it called to mind Saint Anthony and all the other pieces of saints I had seen. Perhaps it was a renewed interest in all that is implied by the word *miracle*; or perhaps it was the experience of seeing the component parts of a human being in a state of existence that was somewhere in between, not fully in the world and not fully out of it. Either way, I thought of relics and all the living souls who had lined up to be in their presence. People are drawn to relics, I realized, because they make explicit what we all know in our own bones: that bodies tell stories; that the transformation offered by faith is not just about, as the Gospels put it, the "word made flesh," but the flesh made word. Behind the glass of every reliquary is a life story told in still frame. That was what I saw on the ultrasound screen as well. What we were, what we will become, all there behind the glass.

I looked again at the fragile lines that represented the bones of my daughter, the frame of all she will be and know. *These bones*, I thought, *these bones are where belief begins.*

What my wife and I will teach our children about faith is a series of open questions. Yet, as I studied my first child for the first time, I already knew that I wanted her to know about the great variety of beliefs in the world she would soon enter. I wanted her to know how lucky she is to be born at a time when a vast spiritual vocabulary is open to her. I wanted to teach her that faith is strange and beautiful and sometimes scary.

Of course, in order to teach one must first learn. And so, just as I was preparing for fatherhood—a time when one is particularly concerned with life—I conceived of undertaking a journey that to my friends and family must have seemed oddly obsessed with death. One week here, two weeks there, I set off to explore the universe of relics, making sure to be home far more often than I was away, always thinking about the intersections of bodies and faith in our lives and in the world. As much as one can ever make sense of one's own pre-occupations, I suppose I found in this period of expectation, waiting for the arrival of a child, something similar to what I felt when faced with pieces of saints, a feeling that life and death are not always black and white. The stubborn vitality of relics, like the awful fragility of the earliest moments of life, suggests that between all we know of living and all we fear of dying there is vast gray space in which we can hope only to make sense of it all.

＊

TO BE DECLARED a saint or holy person in almost any religious tradition has elements of a curse as well as a blessing: it is to guarantee that your body—or a body said to be yours—will be cut apart, inspected, bickered over, and sent around the world. Yet, in every case, these parts—toes, hands, ribs, hair— are important precisely because of the whole person they had been. I wanted to understand the phenomenon of religious relics by undoing what history has done to them. I wanted to piece them back together, to build a composite of the range of relic veneration by assembling a full image of the body, from toes to whiskers with a jumble of bones in between.

During my travels I was particularly drawn to those arti-facts that have maintained their relevance, often in unexpected ways. What *relevance* can mean, unfortunately, is that people often fight and die over many of the relics discussed in this book. To grapple with relics is to know the worst, and maybe also the best, that religion offers the world.

If I was a praying man, I might beseech Saint Anthony, patron saint of both lost things and those in search of elo-quence, to help me find the words to make this so. My use for prayer comes and goes, however. When it comes to look-ing for inspiration, I turn instead to stories. One that I heard while waiting to see the holy tongue all those years ago has stayed with me: It seems Saint Anthony was hearing confessions one day when a man came and told him that he'd had an argument with his mother and kicked her before storming out of the house. Saint Anthony said to him, "Any foot that would kick the mother who made it should be cut off!" The power of the tongue that spoke these words was so great that the man went home, grabbed his ax, and chopped off his foot. When Anthony heard about this he knew he had to be more careful with his words. The tongue God had given him—the relic I would one day see behind glass in Saint Anthony's basilica—was capable of doing as much harm as good. He went to the man immediately and talked the foot into rejoining the leg, by faith repairing the damage that faith had done.

I

CATCH A MARTYR
BY THE TOE

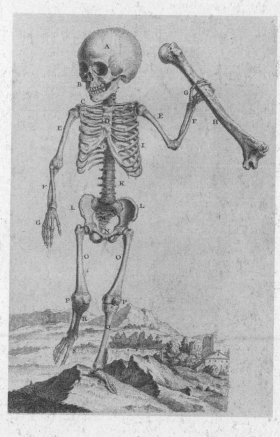

W<small>E KNOW THE WORLD THROUGH OUR BODIES: THE SMELL</small> of it, the taste of it, the weight and the sting. Today I know it first through my ears.

It's Christmas, and even before I wake fully my head is filled with the sounds of singing at once foreign and familiar. Muted hymns, far-off carols. Some of the words I know, but their cadence I do not. A few of the melodies I have hummed since before I knew the reason they were sung, yet the syllables marking the notes come now as if in the language of dreams, their meaning caught only in pieces.

Other parts of my body follow my ears to life: My eyes open to the painted white planks of a ceiling built two hundred years before my country was born. My spine strains against the metal bed beneath me, barely cushioned by the one-inch mattress my hosts no doubt consider an extravagance reserved for guests. Finally, my feet touch down on the cool tile floor and I make my way to the open window, where my nose encounters the scents of bougainvillea and livestock, urine and incense and a hint of sage. My skin feels the wind already blowing hot, though the sun has barely lit the sky. The soft tissues inside my skull somehow put all of this together, and I remember:

I am in India.

I am in Goa, in a coastal region of the subcontinent where at this time of year the serpentine streets are clogged with shirtless Europeans and Israelis racing from beaches to raves on rented scooters, where temples and churches alike are haunted by ninety-pound beggars calling for coins, where the ruins of a failed colony are littered with the plastic bottles and junk-food wrappers of a growing economic giant. I am here to see a man about a toe.

Several toes, in fact: one toe that is no longer there and a few that remain. Together these toes tell a story of religious obsession and the mutual transformation of the living and the dead. They were not the first religious relics—not by a long shot—but they might have been the first with global reach. They are toes that were born in Europe, died in Asia, and came to be enshrined here on the Arabian Sea, a hundred yards from where I was sleeping, where each morning the man they once belonged to is greeted with a liturgy in a language that he never understood and I do not know either.

Outside my door, my accidental guide to Goa is waiting for me.

"The Mass has just ended," Brother Shannon says. "Now the tourists will come."

✳

THAT TOES COULD become a tourist attraction simply by being displayed should not come as a surprise. The lure of relics—the macabre magnetism that makes us look despite what may seem like good manners—is perhaps the most peculiar way in which religion can transcend time and culture. No one can say for certain when the practice of saving and venerating the remains of those sometimes called "the holy dead" be-gan, but it is likely older than any other religious practice that has survived until today. It is unknown if funeral rites preceded relic veneration, or vice versa, but as the existence of one led naturally to the other, the question of whether ritualized mourning led to the creation of relics or if the creation of relics led to ritualized mourning is a prehistoric chicken and egg question never to be answered.

Some of what is known about the history of preserving pieces of the dead for spiritual reasons is this: The Greeks did it as part of their religious devotion to soldiers killed in battle. The Jivaro people of the Amazon did it to harness the power of their enemies. The Egyptians did it for kings whom they called gods, while the people of pre-Buddhist Japan did it to themselves, developing a method of self-mummification that resulted in once-living statues worshipped as images of eternity. From the ostensibly secular world: In Moscow, the Kremlin put Lenin on display and kept teams of morticians busy attempting to posthumously maintain his propaganda-poster-boy good looks. In Beijing, Chairman Mao got the same treatment. Closer to home, a museum in Georgia has enshrined "Possibly Elvis's Toenail," found deep in the shag carpet of Graceland's Jungle Room.

Relics are found in every corner of the earth and at various stages of the development of human culture. What these practices have in common is the transformation of a life into an object, turning something once useful only to an individual into something useful for an entire community.

The usefulness of these objects is the key to understanding—or rather imagining—their origins. Anthropologists suggest that the seeds of relic veneration may have been present even before the dawn of religion, at the earliest sites of human burial. Archaeological evidence suggests that Neanderthals first decided to put the dead into the ground about seventy thousand years ago. On the face of it, this is a very strange thing to do—a bad decision even by Neanderthal standards. The dead, after all, are dangerous. Stinking, full of disease, attractive to large predators, they would be far better burned, thrown off a cliff, or left behind to rot and be eaten on the forest floor. Yet somewhere in our species' earliest prehistory, we decided it would be a good idea to have access to the dead. Could it be that Neanderthals began to bury bodies in well-defined places because they might need the bones later on?*

The answer to the next logical question—need them for what?—begins to explain what could possibly make pieces of dead flesh attractive to the living. Relics came to be regarded as useful not just as mementos of those who had passed on, but as uniquely powerful objects in their own right. Just as our ancestors learned to use a stone tied to a stick as a cudgel, relics began to be collected because they were seen as tools.

Like burial, rumors of the power of the dead occur very early in humanity's religious history. Though Judaism is one of the few religions that does not officially venerate relics,

---

* The work of some primatologists may actually push the desire for relics back before the birth of the species. Barbara J. King, author of *Evolving God: A Provocative View on the Origins of Religion*, told me recently that apes studied in captivity have displayed mourning practices. When a member of an ape community dies, the surviving members need to see, and touch, the body before they are able to get on with their lives. They do not go so far as to tear off a piece of the fallen ape as a keepsake.

even the Hebrew scriptures speak of the supernatural power of bones. In the second book of Kings, the story is told of the prophet Elisha's remains. Long after his death, a corpse was accidentally dropped into the prophet's tomb. "When the body touched Elisha's bones, the man came to life and stood up on his feet" (2 Kings 13:21). Elsewhere in early Hebrew writing it is said, "In his life he did great wonders, and in death he wrought miracles" (Sirach 48:15).

It's easy to see why some would get a bit carried away by the chance to claim a small piece of holiness, even if it comes in the shape of a toe.

✳

SAINT FRANCIS XAVIER, original owner of the toes I have come to Goa to see, was one of the most successful failures who ever lived. Sent from what was then the heart of Christendom to convert India, Japan, and China, he had long-term results that can be seen in the tiny Christian populations of each of these countries today. His short-term results were even worse.

After a pampered upbringing in a castle named for his family in the Navarre region of Spain, Francis set out for Paris in 1525 to receive an education. While there, he fell off the usual course set for noblemen of the era when he left worldly schooling behind to follow a charismatic preacher called Ignatius, who would later found the Jesuit order of Catholic priests. Francis was among his first acolytes, and his most gung ho.

Jesuits today are regarded as the intellectual elite of the Roman Catholic Church. When the order was founded, they thought of themselves more as its ground troops. Ignatius of Loyola famously summed up his faith, and that of the men who would follow him, with this masterful bit of Orwellian thinking, four hundred years before Orwell was born: "I will believe that the white I see is black if the hierarchical Church so defines it." Francis Xavier was fully on board for this approach to the faith. Neither a leader like Ignatius, nor a spiritual genius like the more famous Saint Francis—the animal-loving mystic from Assisi who founded the Franciscans—Francis Xavier became best known for his willingness to go where he was told, no questions asked.

This was a time when Christendom was in full bloom. When Francis was born, the Dark Ages had passed; the Black Death was a grandmother's memory. The age of exploration had barely begun: just fourteen years before, Columbus had spotted land in the islands that would later be called the Bahamas. In response, Pope Alexander VI proclaimed that the world should be divided between the two Catholic superpowers of the time. With a line drawn down the middle of the Atlantic, three hundred miles west of the Cape Verde Islands, all that was soon to be called the New World was declared the property of Spain; all lands uninhabited by Christians east of the line would belong to Portugal. Since it was the pope who was doing the dividing, what this really meant was that all the world belonged to Rome. Oblivious to the Reformation lurking just around the corner, and to the fact that it was about to splinter from within, the Catholic Church began to look outward, hoping to spread the faith to the far corners of the earth.

Born in Spain, Francis might have been destined for the West. At Ignatius's suggestion, however, his most eager pupil was sent to India as representative of both the church and the Portuguese crown. His was the first such extended mission into the world Europeans then knew only as "the Orient." Later reports would claim that he brought about thousands of conversions, but modern historians dispute this. The truth is that during his life he broke little new ground.

It's not hard to see why: he didn't exactly go out of his way to ingratiate himself to the locals. By all accounts (his own and others), Francis Xavier, the future patron saint of India, did not much like Indians. Later, when writing back home for new recruits, he stressed that he had no need for strong minds; strong backs were all he required, "that they may bear the fatigue of continual baptizing and teaching, and going about, as they will often have to do, not only to baptize new born children, but to protect the Christians from the fury and rage of the heathen."

Francis wanted men who could put up with the hardships of trekking into the countryside to convert a reluctant people—work that was made especially difficult as his missionaries did not travel light. They carried food and other gifts to give when the Christian sacraments were accepted but had to defend these wares when the locals declined salvation. Of his new home in Goa, Francis Xavier wrote back to Ignatius:

"Robbery is so public and common here that it hurts no one's character, and hardly counts as a fault: people scarcely hesitate to think that, what is done with impunity, it cannot be bad to do. Everywhere, and all times, it is rapine, hoarding, and robbery."

He never allowed a single local to join the Jesuit order, believing that they, unlike other groups he would later try to convert, lacked the capacity for reason. After only a short time on the subcontinent, he seemed to sense that he was facing a lost cause. He set out to redeem himself by heading farther east. When he left Goa for the last time, he groaned all the while about the thieving nature of the place and the people who lived there. "No one here thinks of making restitution of what he has once taken," he complained. "The devices by which the heathens rob, the various pretexts under which it is done, who can count?" He would've been surprised to know who would later steal his bones.

*

BROTHER SHANNON, a rail-thin, boyish-looking man of thirty, is the junior member of a very small religious community. Built to house as many as one hundred priests, Goa's Jesuit residence is now home to only five. Its ten-foot-wide, whitewashed stairwells twist up four stories from the plaza below to the empty dormitory on the top floor. The hallways still seem to echo with the comings and goings of the Portuguese clerics who once held sway over the city. The building is still called the Casa Professa, the house of the professed, as those who had made professions of faith to the order gathered here to learn all that such a commitment would entail.

Those days are over. The city now is dotted with the ruins of a colonial Christian past, which in the sixteenth and seventeenth centuries transformed Goa from a sleepy fishing town to a briefly bustling hub of international commerce. Today, stone churches crumble among garbage piles and packs of stray dogs. Inside the basilica, there are more signs that an era has ended. During my stay with Goa's Jesuits, the once vibrant community life is limited to quiet and hurried mealtimes, when the four priests, one priest-in-training, and occasional guests gather in the refectory beneath a clock that chimes "It's a Small World After All" every day at noon.

As a Goan Catholic, Brother Shannon grew up hearing stories of Francis Xavier and knew from an early age that he wanted to be a priest. Yet there is nothing sanctimonious about this brother. Only his somewhat celibate air might suggest he is weaving himself into a man of the cloth. His main work is with the community's youth ministry, for which he plays guitar and sings folkie hymns to groups of students from Catholic schools throughout the province. A product of such education, he played basketball for the team of a nearby Jesuit high school and came to know all he knows about America by reading about the NBA in the school's random assortment of U.S. periodicals. Given this, and his age, it does not come as a surprise to discover that Brother Shannon seems to regard Chicago—home of Michael Jordan's Bulls, unbeatable in the years of Shannon's youth—as the cultural capital of America. The city where I live now—Washington, D.C.—is to him far less interesting. My hometown of Boston, I'm glad to say, does at least warrant a smile of recognition.

"Ah, yes," Shannon says. "Larry Bird."

Brother Shannon's home, the Basilica of Bom Jesu ("Good Jesus"), of which the Casa Professa is a part, is the most popular tourist attraction in the tourism capital of India. That doesn't mean that it brings in more sightseers than the Taj Mahal, but the numbers are much larger than would be expected for a not terribly impressive church far from a sizable Christian population. Though it is India's smallest state, Goa hosts nearly 20 percent of its tourists over the course of the year. Most come for the beaches, but as many as two hundred thousand annually come to see what remains of its patron saint.

My room at the basilica overlooks a lush green courtyard where I can watch visitors come and go. There are some who have come from far away—Europeans and Americans in shorts and T-shirts—but far more are local; many of them have been here hundreds of times. They take their shoes off as they enter the church, holding flip-flops or loafers or high heels prayerfully before their chests with one hand as they snap cell phone pictures with the other.

"Ninety percent of the visitors here are Hindu," Brother Shannon tells me. "They take their shoes off because that is what they do at the Hindu temple."

Indian pilgrims to a Portuguese church, they come because they consider the man around whom the church is built to be holy, no matter that his beliefs sought to see theirs snuffed out.

On their way into the church, the Hindu pilgrims crowd around a garishly lit nativity set, a succinct articulation of these apparent contradictions. Flashing the same red, green, blue, and orange lights often seen in the local Hindu temples, it depicts a scene set in Bethlehem, but it has been decorated with balls of cotton that make it seem as if a New England winter storm has taken the plastic camels by surprise. Around the edges, little piles of food and trinkets form a partial wall; these are gifts for Jesus, offered in true Hindu fashion.

All the while, now that Mass has ended, the hymns that woke me have been replaced by Western Christmas music— actually, a disorienting mélange of the Indian *idea* of Western Christmas music—piped in through speakers arranged around the church grounds for the holiday. Unlike the earlier liturgy, which sounded familiar though it was in the local Konkani language, these carols are like none I've heard before. Waves of cultural references wash over the already muddy scene: there are techno beats added to the smooth crooning of Bing Crosby; a disco remix made of the oatmeal tones of Burl Ives; and the surprise of mariachi music as 1950s country singer Jim Reeves's deep voice sings a song about asking "Señor Santa Claus" for a peso to buy something for his señorita. "Christmas music, yes?" Brother Shannon says. "Just like at home for you?"

"Not quite," I tell him. This vivid hybridization of cultures must make perfect sense to Shannon, whose very name comes from a similar sort of East-meets-West cultural cross-referencing. His parents used to work in the tourism industry, Shannon tells me, and in the days when they awaited Shannon's birth, his father found himself often looking at a map of Ireland, particularly at the name of the town where its main airport could be found.

For the locals, the music is part of the attraction. Like

Shannon's father naming him for a European airport he had never seen, the Hindu tourists come both for Francis Xavier and for the West he still represents: distant yet present, something at which to simultaneously gawk, covet, emulate, ponder, and resent. People crowd in through the basilica's three sets of doors and immediately start photographing everything in sight: the chipped windows, the ancient electric fans, the display case of unlabeled relics to the right and left of the altar, and, of course, Francis Xavier's silver and crystal coffin displayed atop a fifteen-foot pedestal in the back corner of the church.

A priest in a white cassock walks through the crowd with a kick in his step and his hands clasped behind his back. Wearing untinted glasses with aviator frames, holding his face in a friendly but no-nonsense smile, he *tsk-tsks* a father snapping a photo of his children, nodding to a sign that in three languages declares such things forbidden.

"Do you see there? The sign says, 'No taking pictures of persons.' Only the church take pictures of, right?"

The priest, Father Savio, is the rector of the basilica. In addition to saying Mass at least once each day, his main responsibility is making sure the rules are followed and the purpose of the church is not too distorted by its inter-religious patronage. He oversees a small team of sextons whose entire job seems to be preventing people from taking photographs of one another. The only person they are allowed to photograph is no longer a person at all, just a collection of dried tissues and crumbling bones set high above the milling crowd. Only the jagged range of his abused feet is visible from below.

There is a significant industry leading the tourists to within photograph range of what is left of Francis Xavier. Each tour guide is a young man gesturing and pointing, followed by a group of three to five visitors. Each group jockeys for position with the others, following a circuit around the basilica that builds to the climax of a glimpse of the saint.

Much of Father Savio's day is filled with moving people along, keeping the crowds from creating a traffic jam as they stand on their tiptoes to get a better look. Father Savio narrows his eyes behind his glasses and walks deliberately toward the mob, his cassock dusting the floor. The tourists see him coming and don't even wait for a word of rebuke; they snap one last photo with their camera phones then hurry on their way.

"It's a terrible problem, the tour guides," Father Savio tells me. "They come in during Mass, talking nonsense. Most of the things they say about Saint Francis Xavier they make up as they go! I heard one explain to a group of Hindus that the remains of the saint are shrinking, and that Catholics believe that when he shrinks to nothing it will be the end of the world."

It is later, beneath the Small World clock in the refectory, that Father Savio recounts his complaint to me, Brother Shannon, and Father Franklin, the superior of the community. Franklin, the oldest among them, sips his tea slowly, with the air of a man who has seen enough not to get too upset over trivialities. His balding pate never creases at the mention of the church's visitors and their unorthodox practices.

"Oh, that is only the beginning," Brother Shannon says. "We have other relics in the church, bones in glass cases which line the front altar. There is no record of who they belong to, but ask the tour guides and they will tell you! They say the bones come from 'Jesuit saints,' but who they have in mind I have no idea. There are more bones there than there have been Jesuits, and not all have been saints."

Father Franklin only smiles at the younger men's vexation.

"I suppose it is a good thing they don't say the bones have come from dinosaurs," he says.

When I ask later if they really do not know whose bones are displayed at the front of the church, Brother Shannon and Father Savio can only shrug. The memory and the myth of Francis Xavier is powerful enough here that the aura of his remains has crowded out any details—either recollected or created—of all the others. Even so, the priests of the Basilica of Bom Jesu do not speak very often of the man whose bones receive endless attention. It is as if to discuss Francis Xavier would be to comment on the air they breathe. Yet the church is here because the saint is here, and so are they.

✳

WHEN FRANCIS LEFT Goa, he went first to Japan, because he believed that, unlike the Indians who had so rudely deflected his evangelizing efforts, the Japanese were "a race greatly given to the exercise of reason."

For a time he also believed he was a great success. With the help of a former samurai he had met and converted at the start of his travels in Japan, Francis had translated and memorized a bit of the Gospels in order to explain himself to the locals. Samurai lived by a code that was nearly a religion in its own right, but it's likely, given the events that followed, that Francis's translator had had some exposure to Buddhism as well. With this help, many prospective converts, particularly those most attached to their own religion, were interested in what Francis had to say. He told everyone he met he was there to teach about *Dainichi*, the word his translator had told him was a close enough approximation of *God*.

As one might expect, Francis Xavier spoke well of Dainichi—so well that a group of Buddhist monks took him in, surprised and intrigued by what he said. During his stay with the monks, he learned that Dainichi was, in fact, one of the many names of the Buddha; he had been attributing all the miracles of the Gospels to the teacher the Japanese already revered. Thereafter Francis tried out other names but met with less success. After the emperor rebuffed repeated attempts to meet with him, Francis set his sights on China, then as now a tempting market for optimistic international conglomerates.

This time he was unable even to enter the kingdom. He made it only as far as a coastal island, where a merchant had promised, after collecting a considerable sum of money as an advance for his services, that he would rendezvous with Francis and smuggle him to the mainland.

It was there, in a thatch hut, waiting for transport that would never come, that Francis Xavier died after a short illness. He had been a college dropout, a lousy missionary, a vocal anti-Indian racist. Some I met in Goa called him a proto-colonialist, a Catholic supremacist, an imperialist stooge. As of December 3, 1552, he was a corpse ten thousand miles from home at a time when such a journey would take a year or more.

That might have been the end of a rather unremarkable cleric with three failed missions on his résumé, but then something happened. Out of respect for his role in a religious order growing in popularity and power, a passing ship captain arranged for Francis's remains to be transported back to his Jesuit confreres. Yet conditions aboard ocean vessels were bad enough without bringing a rotting corpse along. So, as was the custom in circumstances like this, Francis's body was placed in a ditch in the island sand and covered with quicklime, which increased the rate of decomposition, reducing a body to bones in a period of weeks. In a few months, if anyone still had an interest in sending Francis home, he would likely be in a more travel-ready state.

After enough time had elapsed, the order came to unearth the missionary's remains. When his fellow Jesuits dug down into the grave, however, they found a surprising thing: Francis. All of him. Not bones but a full body, like a proud papa who lets his children bury him in the sand then looks up smiling when they uncover him. Francis had lain six feet under for months and was still quite dead, but as fresh as the moment he took his last breath. His body was, as Catholics had begun to say of others who were so saintly they did not decompose, incorrupt.

This was exciting news, at least for those on the right side of the lime pit—which is to say those staring down and not up. For Francis, meanwhile, it was par for the course. Even in death, he had failed to do what was expected of him.

✳

OF COURSE, FRANCIS Xavier's failure during life is not unique among saints. The history of Christian holy men and women is filled with failures. It could even be said that a certain kind of failure was for a time required as a sign of sanctity. Saints had to be reviled, they had to be scorned, at times they had to be killed, just as surely as prophets had been biblically required to go unrecognized among their own people. In the early days of Christianity, the struggling religion was so intent on making the case that worldly success did not matter that it made a fetish of its opposite. Failure was humbling, after all, and humility was the road to glory.

Take the first documented case of Christian relic veneration, for example: Saint Polycarp, burned at the stake in AD 155. At the height of the "age of martyrs," Polycarp, the feisty eighty-six-year-old bishop of the Christian community of Smyrna, on Turkey's western coast, was brought before a hooting mob and asked to deny his faith. The stadium still bore the marks of previous rounds of this Roman blood sport. Not long before, according to a contemporary account, other Christians had met their ends by means of "wild beasts . . . sharp shells . . . and other forms of manifold tortures."

Because they denied the existence of all Roman gods, followers of Jesus were then known as atheists, and so when Polycarp was asked to recant his Christianity, it was the words "Away with the atheists" that his interrogator wanted to hear. Polycarp looked to heaven, swept his hand in the direction of the pagan crowd, and called forth divine wrath: "Away with the atheists!" Not us, he told them, you.

If the Romans flinched upon hearing the holy man call

down fury upon them, they recovered quickly. Neither lightning bolts nor plagues followed the old bishop's words. The only visible fire of judgment came when they lit a pyre at Polycarp's feet.

The Romans watched for a while as the flames rose around him, but apparently it was taking too long. Soon an executioner was dispatched to stab Polycarp with a dagger. In a few minutes he was dead.

But that was just the beginning of the story. When news of the bishop's death reached the Christians of Smyrna, it was not the fact of his martyrdom but the process by which it had been accomplished, and the alleged physical transformations it entailed, that most excited them. Polycarp's coreligionists quickly elaborated on the known details of the story: "The fire, making the appearance of a vault, like the sail of a vessel filled by the wind, made a wall round about him. The body was there in the midst, not like flesh burning, but like a loaf in the oven, or like gold and silver refined in a furnace. For we perceived such a fragrant smell, as if it were the wafted odor of frankincense or some other precious spice."

As the Christians told the tale, it was only upon seeing this that the Romans rushed in to stab the saint. And even then, according to one legend, such a torrent of blood was released from Polycarp's wound that the flames were extinguished. Another version of the legend says that along with a fountain of blood, a dove flew into the air.

Not only had his flesh not burned, it had been perfected by the fire. In life, the old bishop had not been a miracle worker, only a teacher. Somehow the act of dying had made him something new.

Hearing this, the Christians of Smyrna rallied around the cause of getting the holy body back. By then, the idea of martyrdom was well established in the young religion. Before Polycarp's execution, a martyr's death had spoken mainly of the courage of the life that preceded it. Now it seemed dying itself could make a holy man holier still. With Polycarp, a new innovation sprang up. His followers didn't just want his memory; they wanted his bones. They gathered them up with the belief that they were "more precious than pearls, more tried than gold." After Polycarp—his flesh attaining a golden glow "like a loaf in the oven" rather than charring black—the saint's body became an essential part of the saint's story. At times it became the most important part: remains, by their definition, remain. They offer a constancy to which no human life—nor even memory—can aspire.

The cult of relics spread quickly. At first undoubtedly a fringe movement of a fringe faith, by the third century enough relics had been collected that many of that era survive today. By the fourth century, acceptance for the veneration of relics was such that Gregory of Nyssa could remark of the so-called Forty Martyrs, Christian soldiers killed in battle in the Armenian city of Sebaste only a few years before, "their ashes and all that the fire had spared have been so distributed throughout the world that almost every province has had its share of the blessing. I also myself have a portion of this holy gift and I have laid the bodies of my parents beside the ashes of these warriors, that in the hour of the resurrection they may be awakened together with these highly privileged comrades."

It remains to be seen what resurrection may look like for someone who has been distributed to "almost every province," but this much is clear: by just its third century of existence, Christianity had turned bones and ashes into commodities comparable to gems and precious metals, except only more precious. More important for the story of Francis Xavier, the remains of the holy dead had become emissaries in their own right, sent as reminders of the faith to outposts in far-off lands.

Perhaps inevitably, as relics increased in number and became more widespread, there arose a need to categorize and classify them. Within Catholicism there came to be three distinct kinds: first class, second class, and third class, with further scales of value evident but less formally defined within each class. First-class relics include any object that may have had contact with Jesus Christ during his life, death, or resurrection: wood from the stable where legend says he was born; pieces of the cross or nails used for his crucifixion; the Shroud of Turin, which the faithful believe wrapped his body as it was set in the tomb. Other first-class relics include all or a portion of the body of a saint. If the body part was deemed "important" to the saint's life or work,* it was considered all the more valuable. For example, the finger with which John the Baptist pointed to

---

* An interesting distinction, as it is hard to imagine even the holiest saint getting by without a spleen, and yet that is not quite the import of *important* here. In the case of relics, a body part is considered more valuable if it plays a role in stories or legends of the saint. Hence, the tongue of the great orator Saint Anthony is a higher-grade relic than his earlobe might be.

Jesus when he said "Behold the man" is enshrined in a church in Florence and is regarded as one of the most important relics in all of Italy (which is saying quite a lot considering the number of first-class relics in Rome alone). As a saint's flesh that also played a role in Christ's life, it is, in a sense, a first-class relic to the second power. Second-class relics are nearly as prized. These are anything associated with the saint's life that was not a flesh-and-bone part of that life. Had John the Baptist worn a watch, for example, it would be a second-class relic. (Had Jesus given it to him, it would be a first.) A third-class relic is anything—anything at all—that has touched a first-class relic. These different classes of relics ensured that there was truly no end to the number of relics that could be in the world, to the places that the faith could be spread with them, or the churches that could be founded around them. Seen charitably, this meant that anyone could aspire to possess one. Seen cynically—and no less historically—the three-classes scheme meant that counterfeiting of the second and third classes could be easily performed, and that the value of the original articles—the bodies themselves—increased exponentially.

Such valuable items were not without their own mixed blessings. At times the death of the holiest would become welcome for an unholy reason: saints were now worth more dead than alive.

✳

FRANCIS XAVIER HAD only faith in common with Polycarp. His death came without the drama of stadiums and persecution. He was an agent of empire, not a target of it. Yet when news of his refusal to decay began to spread, his remains were treated with the same kind of fervor. What had happened in the millennium and a half between one saint's death and another's was essentially a transformation of the meaning of Christianity.

As followers of a religion of protest, Christians in Polycarp's age were regarded as atheists by the ruling pagans. By the time Francis was tromping through the wilds of Goa, the tables had turned. Christianity and worldly power had become synonymous. The bodies of saints no longer had to defy the rulings of temporal authority. Now if they were to serve a symbolic purpose they had to defy something more powerful than that. Namely, death itself.

At the time of Francis's death, incorruptibility was all the rage. During the fifteenth and sixteenth centuries, more saints were found not to decay than any before or since. In Italy, Saint Catherine of Bologna was declared incorrupt and then displayed sitting up with a prayer book in her lap, as she remains today. So many candles were placed around her that her skin eventually took on a brownish hue, as if she had been slow-roasted in her open tomb. Saint Rita of Cascia, Blessed Margaret Castello, Saint Cecilia, and other holy women who had died long before were "discovered" to be incorrupt around this same time.

The earlier church had had no use for such things. They might keep the bones of saints, but the notion that faith could stop the process of death and decay altogether did not arise until much later. Only after the church had gathered significant earthly power did it began to ask of its saints that they not decompose.

Even at the time, incorruptibility was hard for some to accept. When the "whole and fresh" body of Francis was shipped off from that desolate island on the Chinese coast, he had the bad luck, according to some accounts, of ending up on board the ship of a Portuguese merchant who had no love for Jesuits. Long before reaching the planned-for destination, Francis was off-loaded. At the direction of the ship captain, he was removed from his coffin and laid in a shallow ditch by the locals. Then they beat him to a pulp. As a contemporary report explains: "As is the custom in Malacca, they pounded the body with long pestles in such a manner that they made big lesions in some parts and broke the bones of the collar, knee and other parts of the body. In this state it remained buried for some months."

Once again that should have been the end of Francis Xavier. However, as it happened, Malacca was at the time in the grip of a plague. Soon after pounding Francis into the ground, the Malaccans began to notice that the number of plague cases had declined. Locals attributed this to the missionary they had so recently pulverized and buried on the beach. One might suppose that the Malaccans hoped such a miracle-making inhabitant would remain among, or at least under, them but soon enough the Jesuits also heard of the miracle and came looking for their man.

On December 11, 1553, Francis was again disinterred and loaded onto a boat, this time bound for India. Even before the boat was tied up at the port, word of the incorrupt— if broken—body spread through the city he had been so happy to leave behind. Crowds gathered at the dock in hopes of catching a glimpse of the body that some were already calling not just a saint but *Goencho Saib*, "The Lord of Goa."

*

ON MY THIRD day at the basilica, Brother Shannon informs me I am to be joined in the Casa Professa's guest rooms by a group of fifty-five preteens: boys and girls from one of dozens of schools in India that bear Xavier's name.

"Come," Brother Shannon says, "they will want to meet you."

They are from a northern city where Catholic culture is far less prevalent than it is in Goa. Catholics there are a tiny minority, one of the teachers tells me, and so though it is a Catholic school, only ten of the fifty-five students are Christian. The rest are Hindus, Muslims, Jains—the usual spiritual grab bag in a nation that is rivaled only by the United States in its religious diversity. No matter their faith, the teacher says, all of the students are excited to see the body of the man for whom their school is named.

"You will see when you meet them, many of the students who are not Catholic ask, 'Where is the mummy?'" Brother Shannon says. "It is not just children who say this. The Hindus who come to the church all the time are saying, 'I want to see the mummy!' We must then explain it is not a mummy. It is the holy relics of a saint."

When I hear the students making their way up the steps of the Casa Professa, I guess that they will be excited to see anything, be it mummy or saint or just the statue of Saint Francis that greets them at the top of the stairs. Eleven to fourteen years old, they charge forward in twos and threes to pose with the statue giving thumbs-up, sticking out their tongues, crossing their eyes while their teachers and friends snap pictures. For many this is their first trip away from home and it matters little that they are staying in a church; they are seeing the world, nearly bursting with the excitement of it.

"This is Mister Peter who is here to learn about the relics of Saint Francis Xavier," Brother Shannon announces, and immediately I have fifty-five sets of eyes on me. They stare as if there is some vital piece of information missing from the introduction.

"Mister Peter has come all the way from the United States," Brother Shannon adds, "so we will welcome him most kindly."

"Ah!" fifty-five middle schoolers exclaim. "America!"

They eye me with a mix of wonder and suspicion as we climb aboard their tour bus and begin to make our way around the sites of Goa. It takes forty-five minutes for the most adventurous among them to saunter up and say, "Hello, Mister Peter! How do you do!" Then the floodgates open: "Hello! Hello!" they shout and then scurry away, all of them searching for something else to say.

Finally, a boy in a Spider-Man T-shirt inches his way forward. His overlarge sunglasses give him the appearance of a miniature superhero himself.

"Are you Peter Parker?" Spider-Man asks.

Laughter and shouting fill the bus, and there is immediate agreement that I must be. The tone is set for the rest of my time among them.

"Please be respectful of Mister Peter," one of the teachers

says. "He is here for a noble purpose. Didn't Brother Shannon tell you he is here to learn about the relics of Saint Francis Xavier as you are?"

"Spider-Man has come to see the mummy!" another small boy shouts.

"Remember what we learned in school," the teacher says. "The basilica does not hold a mummy but the incorrupt relics of a saint."

"What does *incorrupt* mean?"

"It means he is all there, head to toe. He has not been burned like most people when they die."

"It means he is a mummy!"

"Not a mummy!"

"What do you think, Peter Parker? Is it a mummy or saint?"

"Can't it be both?" I ask.

Mummy or no, the kids are clearly in awe when their teachers lead them into the basilica to see what is left of the saint. Faced with the ornate glass and silver casket, half hidden behind a curtain of fine gold chain, they stand with their mouths and eyes open wide, their necks tilted so far back it seems as though they are looking at the stars.

After a few minutes they begin looking at one another instead, then lifting pointed fingers and flashing huge grins, uncertain what to do next. Finally, one of the teachers produces a camera and snaps a photo of the casket. As if they didn't know this would be allowed, the children immediately drop to their knees—not in prayer but to dig through their backpacks, searching for cameras, which a moment later are propped like third eyes against their heads. The flashes that follow reflect off the glass of the coffin and create the effect of a sudden lightning storm.

The church is still sparkling when I glance around to find a student or two to ask what they think of the saint. Before I can ask, one of the girls in the group is at my side, and she has a question for me: "Do you speak Hindi?"

Her name is Jackpreth, and she is the tallest girl in class, even taller than most of the boys. The boldness with which she approached me suggests she is the most confident as well.

"No," I say. "I don't."

Her eyes grow wide, as if I must be joking. "Not one word?!"

"Not one."

She looks like she's about to let me have it for my ignorance when the boy in the Spider-Man T-shirt rushes up to join us. He is a Hindu and so is especially excited by the other stops they made on their tour of Goa, which included at least a half dozen well-known temples.

"Are you also happy to see the body of the man for whom your school is named?" I asked.

"Oh, yes!"

"What do you think of it?" I asked. "Of seeing the body?"

"Strang—" he starts to say, but his voice trails off, as if suddenly distrusting his English.

"Strange?" I ask.

"*Strength*," Spider-Man says. "The strength of God."

We look up to the casket glowing with electric light, reflecting back at us every time someone tries to preserve the memory. The pulsing strobe effect illuminates the contents of the casket, though from where we stand we can see only the jagged mountain range that was once the saint's foot.

"Teacher said he was all there," Jackpreth says, "but where are his toes?"

*

IF FRANCIS XAVIER truly was incorrupt when he reached Goa, he did not stay that way for long. No sooner was his whole and fresh body on dry land than his new and most enduring role began: religious commodity. And like all commodities, he was alternately hoarded, spent, and stolen.

During the first exposition of the body, in the hot Goan March of 1554, contemporary sources report that a "pious Portuguese woman" living in Goa became so caught up in the excitement of being in the presence of an incorrupt corpse that she could not keep herself from corrupting it.

Leaning in to kiss the saint's feet, she opened her mouth, closed her teeth around the end of his left foot, and bit with force sufficient to remove a chunk of skin and bone. Legend reports that she made off with a little toe, but to look closely at the foot now—with at least three digits missing—is to wonder if she got away with an even bigger bite.

No matter the prize, it was an unreasonable thing to do. And yet, what could state more succinctly the power of relics? Her faith met his faith, and in that union an act so far from the acceptable order of society seemed like a profoundly good idea. I thought of this "pious Portuguese woman" each morning as I ate breakfast with the Jesuits. A seaside region, a fishing economy before the tourists started to arrive, Goa is a place where seafood is eaten three meals a day. Each morning at breakfast in the Casa Professa I would find five tiny dried fish—still complete with skin, flesh, and eyes—waiting on a plate beside my coffee cup. To bite into the crispy skin and through the tiny bones within while hearing the tales of Francis's dismemberment was to dine delicately and deliciously while pondering the extremities of faith, the reasons it makes us do the outlandish things we do. Yes, the pious Portuguese woman was likely crazy as well as devout. But then again, I had traveled halfway around the world to see what was left of the toes she tasted. Which of us was unreasonable?

In any event, the loss of his toes was only the beginning of the ongoing long division of Francis Xavier. In 1614, his right arm was cut at the elbow and his forearm divided into two parts: one sent to Italy for the benefit of the Jesuits of the Church of Gesu, the other sent to Belgium. Five years later, the rest of the arm was removed and sent to Jesuits in Japan. Next went the shoulder blade, which was likewise divided for the use of multiple parties. Two of the three pieces of his upper arm have since been lost, but one remains on display at St. Joseph's Seminary of Macao.

In 1636 came perhaps the single greatest harvest: all of Francis's viscera were removed and divided into dozens of pieces for distribution around the world. Ever after, believers far from where he was born, traveled, or died could see for themselves a little piece of incorruptibility. Even in the latter half of the twentieth century, flakes of his no-longer-whole-and-fresh skin were from time to time scraped off and placed in reliquaries of their own.

Buried four times, beaten with clubs, doused with lime, Francis Xavier's first years after death were nothing like the first pampered years of his life. But it was not all indignity for the Lord of Goa. He did have a lavish basilica built for his final resting place. His remains have made his church among the most widely visited grave sites in the world.

For Goa, he is not just a saint. He is an industry. In the knickknack shop across the street from the basilica they sell the usual Catholic bric-a-brac as well as only-in-Goa items such as clear plastic caskets with a small pink man inside. Among the postcards available for purchase there is, as there must be, a color photo of a foot that looks like it has been gnawed by a hamster.

Outside the basilica gate, vendors push candles and postcards and "hand-carved" plastic portable chess sets painted the color of wood. They also sell wax figurines depicting a child, or a woman, or a head, an arm, a hand, a leg, etc. The feet, with all the usual toes, are among the biggest sellers. It is the practice among some of the faithful in Goa to purchase one of these figures for a few rupees and then take it into the church and place it on an altar, or—at lucky moments when the sacristans are not looking—prop it up on the marble pedestal that holds the saint's remains. Despite the church policy of removing the statuettes at the end of each day, it is common to see a handful of these any time you visit the basilica. There is no end to suffering and so there is no end to the practice of seeking its relief.

I ask Father Savio if the church in any way discouraged this custom.

"It is the faith of the people, why discourage it?" he says. "Anyway, most of those leaving the wax figures are Hindus, not Catholics. If it was Catholics doing this perhaps the church could say something. But when it is Hindus in the church, what can you do?"

Sent to convert the heathen, Francis Xavier has arguably become more an Indian saint than a Catholic one. Whether he is called *mummy* or *incorruptible*, the faithful seem unperturbed that there is not much left of him. From where they stand at the foot of the reliquary, they can still see a toe or two, and that is enough.

✳

THE SUN HAS set by the time the children leave the church. They have had their fill of the mummy, and now they have been instructed to wait in the courtyard while their teachers complete plans for dinner. Several small floodlights click on as the children wait, giving the open area before the church the dramatic appearance of a stage. The more outgoing of the group take to it right away. Soon they are running in clusters of twos and threes, holding hands, the floodlights giving them a larger-than-life feeling.

Jackpreth and Spider-Man again run to my side.

"Mister Peter Parker, we are playing chains! Will you play with us?"

"Chains?"

"First you do not know Hindi, and now you don't know chains?" the tall girl teases. "It is a game we play. Watch, you see? The two holding hands running, they tag a third and together they are a chain. Then they must catch another and make a circle around her. And then she joins the chain."

In death Francis Xavier had joined the lives of a people and a place where he had never wanted to remain. These children, born in the country he scorned, educated in a school that bears his name, have lived their lives in his shadow, but now they run in front of his church, casting their own.

2

PULLING
A LAMA'S LEG

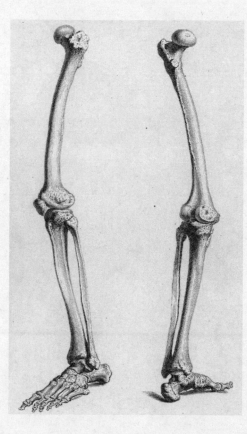

A FEW BLOCKS FROM HOLLYWOOD'S WALK OF FAME, tucked on a side street with a Kentucky Fried Chicken on one corner and a McDonald's on the other, there's a vast warehouse space hidden behind an unassuming glass door. As recently as the late '90s it was a sound studio used for testing the latest developments in audio technology; before that, according to local legend, it was where Elvis kept his California cars, parked under massive redwood beams, in the halo glow of a dozen skylights.

Today the warehouse is a yoga center called Golden Bridge. I have been there only a minute or two when an employee tells me it is the largest facility of its kind in the country. "Although," she admits, "people might just say that the same way they say someone's baby is the cutest in the world. Maybe it's true, maybe not, but does it matter?"

Good question. I've come to Golden Bridge to see a touring exhibition of Buddhist relics: physical remains of the Buddha and a score of other sages and lamas, which believers hold to be material manifestations of enlightenment. For the past five years these relics have been making a circuit of temples and monasteries around the world, with occasional visits to an odd assortment of non-Buddhist communities: a Unity church in Texas, two prisons in Florida, elementary schools throughout the Southwest, and now this Kundalini institute in the shadow of a movie theater and a parking garage.

The relics have come to Golden Bridge because they go pretty much wherever they are invited—so long as the host organization, or some other benefactor, can guarantee that a minimum donation will find its way into the offering box before the exhibit has closed.

The stated aim of the Heart Shrine Relic Tour, according to its promotional brochure, is to spread "a message of loving-kindness and peace" to all who see or hear of it. Yet there is a more practical goal as well. The relics are touring to raise funds for the construction of the largest Buddha sculpture in history: a brass-plated statue fifty stories tall that will loom like a pyramid over an underdeveloped region in northern India called Uttar Pradesh. The Maitreya Buddha figure will stand twice as high as the Statue of Liberty and roughly three times the height of the giant stone Buddhas destroyed by the Taliban in the Bāmiān Valley of Afghanistan in the spring of 2001. Spreading love and peace is also the stated aim of the statue, which according to planners has been "designed to last at least 1,000 years."

It turns out that everlasting loving-kindness on this scale doesn't come cheap. The estimated cost for the Maitreya Project, as the overall construction effort is called, is over $200 million.

And so the relics have their work cut out for them. The tour has made hundreds of stops since its inception. Wherever the relics go, a crowd waits in line, often for hours, to be near the remnants of one of the world's undisputed spiritual titans. They leave with teary eyes and goofy grins; sometimes they get back in line and wait to view the relics again. They come for any number of reasons—bad backs, lost jobs, sick pets, gratitude for a new love affair—and go away talking about the vibrations they felt, the visions they had. Many chant a mantra of "I just can't explain what the relics made me feel." In general, though, there is agreement: coming to see the relics has put them in touch with something powerful and, to use a word that both the faithful and the merely curious seem to choose more often than any other, "real."

It is for "real" that they have come, and, after sliding a few bills into the offering box, most seem to leave certain they've gotten their money's worth.

There are plenty of reasons to doubt that items temporarily on display in a yoga studio just south of Sunset and Vine could truly be the remains of a teacher who died in India 2,500 years ago. Yet whether or not the relics are the real thing—actual pieces of the actual founder of a religion currently five hundred million followers strong—they are being used to raise real money. The lock on the offering boxes isn't there to keep the good karma in.

✳

A FRIED CHICKEN breeze blows by when the wind is right. It clouds the entrance with the sweetness of hot meat and cooking fat, expelled from the open door of the KFC kitchen one hundred yards away. Inside Golden Bridge, however, the atmosphere is strictly vegan. Lithe women in linen pants and tank tops form their hands into steeples and bow at the slightest provocation, offering demur whispers of "Namaste" to anyone whose eyes linger too long on their tattooed shoulders. A woman with vines hennaed on her ankles explains that the greeting means, "The god in me salutes the god in you," and each time she says the word *god* her toes curl in emphasis. No one here wears shoes.

Or much of anything, really. Whatever holy pretensions Golden Bridge has (technically it is not a yoga studio but "a spiritual village"*), it is mainly a fitness facility, with hundreds of students who come not to pray but to sweat. They do so in a half dozen cavernous practice rooms, each identified with the name of a city in India. At the rear of the building, through a sliding wood-paneled wall, is Amritsar. Bodh Gaya is off to the left. The workout room upstairs is named for the place Spalding Gray once called "the sexiest sounding town in India": Pune.

There is no room called Kushinigar, but the main hall today is a stand-in for that far-off village near the border of Nepal where the five-hundred-foot Buddha will be built. It is an area untouched by the subcontinent's economic boom. There are no call centers in Kushinigar, no tech start-ups. But soon it will be home to a major tourist attraction, which the project planners insist will be the salvation of the region. When it is finished, all the relics will be brought and enshrined there, in the statue's heart.

Toward the back of the main hall, a plastic, blue-haired Buddha the size of a large child sits atop a throne on a raised platform made of ornate tapestries and four large folding ta-

---

* This was explained to me by one of Golden Bridge's cofounders, Gurmukh, who is something of a celebrity in the yoga world for her instructional videos and DVDs. When she sat down beside me as I was taking notes, I asked her, "So this is your studio?" "We prefer to say it belongs to the universe," she said.

bles. At five feet tall, the centerpiece of the relic display is a 1/100 scale model of the statue planned for Kushinigar.

Several yoga center workers scurry about placing clear glass bowls around the platform's perimeter and filling them with saffron-tinted water, deferring often to a woman crouched down behind the throne. They pepper her with questions— which bowl where? how much water?—but she is focused on the task of Scotch-taping a gold cloth to the base of the tasseled beach umbrella that hangs above the plastic Buddha's head.

When she finally looks up, she gives a harried smile and assures the yoga people that everything looks fine, just fine.

Her name is Carmen Straight. Tall and regal looking, a bit like Glenn Close, with gray-blond hair falling loose to the shoulders of her burgundy robe, she is the authority here, the custodian of the relics. For the past ten months it has been her job to accompany a suitcase full of the devotional objects to each exhibition site and prepare them for public display.

"I had been looking for work," she says, explaining how she came to be guardian of the Buddha's remains. "One day I got an e-mail about the relic tour from someone I didn't know. I almost deleted it."

Instead, she opened it, and now here she is. Each weekend, Carmen and a volunteer assistant, I Fung, a Chinese-born social worker from San Francisco, pull into a new town with the relics in tow. The two women travel in a maroon van inscribed with blessings in yellow Tibetan script and decorated with Buddhist bumper stickers. Several are multicolored bodhisattva decals; one relates the Dalai Lama's best-known quote: "Kindness is the true religion." My favorite, for its subtle enlightened-being wit, reads "My Other Vehicle Is the Mahayana," a joke that requires a working knowledge of Buddhist history and the centuries-old disagreements between schools of practice to understand.*

Inside, the van is packed to the ceiling with everything required for the transformation of a prison classroom, church basement, or yoga studio into a temporary Buddhist shrine: gold tablecloths, Christmas lights, plastic bags of tea candles, an assortment of glass bowls, eight plastic display cases, and the five-foot-tall statue of the Buddha. They also bring the relics themselves: zipped into a soft-sided suitcase covered with a quilt of yellow and blue Tibetan fabrics. When the relics are on the road, they sit strapped into one of the van's rear passenger seats; the plastic Buddha occupies the other seat, riding like an eight-year-old with his feet not quite touching the floor.

All told the Heart Shrine Relic van reminds me, more than anything, of the Scooby-Doo gang's Mystery Machine, with its trippy fonts and metallic pastels catching the Hollywood sun. Yet its more earnest intent is signified by the blessing posted on the spare-tire case: "May anybody who sees, touches, remem-

---

* The short version goes something like this. There are two major schools of Buddhist practice: the Mahayana and the Theravada. Mahayana includes Tibetan and Chinese strains of Buddhism, while Theravada is centered in the countries of Southeast Asia. Theravada is often referred to by members of the Mahayana as the Hinayana tradition, the former (Mahayana) meaning "The Greater Vehicle" and the latter (Hinayana) meaning "The Inferior Vehicle." So the joke of the bumper sticker is that it plays on the "My other car is a Porsche" culture of American highways while simultaneously getting in an implicit jab at an ancient rival. But like the man said, if it takes longer to explain a joke than to tell it, it might not be funny.

bers, talks, or dreams about this car achieve everlasting happiness and have compassion for all living beings."

When the van is on the road, Carmen is always at the wheel. She was, she would later tell me, a lifelong rambler and occasional seeker who in her youth drove from British Columbia deep into Mexico and back again. Until recently she had been a picker and packer of fruit, passing three years on an isolated farm in her native Canada. A self-imposed exile.

"At the time I just couldn't be around people," she says. "Their pain was too apparent to me, too much to handle."

Now, as the custodian of the relics, she sees people all day long. Once the display is set, she takes her position in a straight-back chair and blesses the faithful, one by one, for hours at a stretch. Some reach the end of the queue and drop silently to their knees. Others bow at the waist and whisper to her, as if to the Buddha himself, all that ails them. The Buddha would not be surprised by the kinds of things she hears. Life, after all, is suffering, as he sadly and famously said.

Inside Golden Bridge, Carmen lifts a small golden reliquary as if she is making a toast, then lowers it onto a quaking head. Beneath her hands, a woman in a tie-dye dress trembles, then convulses in tears.

✳

UNLIKE CHRISTIAN RELICS, which tend toward the macabre, Buddhist relics are fairly easy on the eye. They come, for the most part, in the form of small gemlike pebbles, which are said to take shape when a holy person is cremated. They look a bit like Pop Rocks, or the occasional malformed mint one finds in a Tic Tac dispenser, and though they are believed to be the essence of an enlightened soul, they are found in a very physical way: by sifting through the ashes of the recently deceased, looking for some sign that the life lost will endure past death.

For most religious traditions that venerate physical reminders of the righteous, it is the life that gives worth—spiritual and material—to the matter that is left behind. It is this transference of value, from the whole to the parts, that has given us our understanding of what a relic is. In Christian terms, it has always been the saint that makes the relic, a transaction that fostered an idea of holiness as both portable and enduring, which was a notion as responsible as any other for the spread of the faith through the Roman world and beyond.

In Buddhism, however, the appearance of a relic can make a saint. Tibetan legend is full of tales of secret sages who pass their days unrecognized as anyone of importance only to be grieved like kings when jewels found in their ashes reveal them as enlightened beings.

According to Carmen Straight, this still happens today. She tells me of a man who came to see the Heart Shrine Relic Tour in Hong Kong. His wife had died recently and he'd had her cremated. Then, he said, he brought her cremains to the seaside to cast them into the water. As he scooped the ashes from the urn and scattered them into the wind, he saw that they were filled with a rainbow of colored gems, which he heard plop like stones into the water while the rest of the urn's contents flew into the air. At first he was saddened by the loss of evidence of the great saint his wife had been.

"But then I asked him," Carmen says, " 'Do you know what happened? Her enlightenment spread out through the ocean, and now covers the whole world.' Those relics are doing more good where they are than if he had managed to save them."

Which is not to say that there is no special attention granted to the bodies of those already acknowledged as holy. From the beginning, Buddhism, like Christianity, relied on relics of the revered as a source of movable sanctity, calling cards to be sent off with missionaries to distant lands. According to the Mahaparinibbana-sutta, the Buddhist scripture recording the last days of the Buddha, the enlightened one himself sanctioned the veneration of his physical remains. Tradition holds that hair, teeth, and fragments of bone were distributed to various disciples to be enshrined in stupas far and wide.

In no time, there were hundreds, if not thousands, of hairs purported to belong to the Buddha in circulation. As the new faith spread along with these leavings, it just as quickly ran into trouble because of them. The problem was that in the culture from which Buddhism arose, bodily materials such as hair and fingernails were considered to be by-products of the digestive process. They were, in other words, waste materials. At the dawn of Buddhism, relics were seen as excrement by another name.

To get around this perception that the shrines being built

to the emerging religion were literally full of crap, the writers of the sutras undertook a PR campaign declaring that the Buddha was so far above regular human existence that even his waste was holy. The Buddha's shit, in other words, did not stink. Only with this understanding did it become possible for the veneration of Buddhist relics to take place. And without relics of the Buddha and his followers to serve as ambassadors, the faith might not have spread at all.

Historically speaking, then, the appearance of the Buddha's remains in a Hollywood yoga studio is not all that unusual. The very idea of the veneration of Buddhist relics began with the supposition that they would travel. Yet the overall project of the tour remains something new: the conscription of ancient objects of devotion into a modern-day capital campaign. Relic-based fund-raising may be a tradition that goes back to the oldest cathedral in Christendom, but the Heart Shrine Relic Tour is an unusual religious endeavor of this size in using the mystique of relics to appeal to those beyond the faith.

Credit for the idea of building the largest Buddha in history is given to the late Lama Thubten Yeshe. Born in Tibet in 1935, he studied in monasteries there until 1959 when, as he once said, "China kindly told us that it was time to leave Tibet and to meet the outside world."

Having witnessed the end of two millennia of Buddhism in his homeland, Lama Yeshe came to believe it was time for the coming of Maitreya Buddha, also known as the fifth, or future, Buddha, who was expected to appear only when the teachings of the previous Buddha were passing from the earth.

Before his death in 1984, the lama envisioned a concrete counterpart to Maitreya's mystical return but failed to leave specific instructions or plans for his vision.*

The current head of the effort is Lama Zopa Rinpoche, a Nepalese monk. Under his spiritual leadership, the project has made very practical alliances with international architecture and engineering firms. The official statements of their involvement hint at the tensions likely to arise when the requirements of theology must be explained in the language of business.

The lead architects, London-based Aros Ltd., express this disconnect with perfect cant: "Given the complexities of the design of the Maitreya Project, the Aros studio is developing enormous experience in inter-operability and extranet communication." The design company Mott MacDonald, meanwhile, tackles the structural implications of the Maitreya Buddha's thousand-year reign by promising "special studies" of how climate change, extreme winds, and earthquakes are likely to effect steelwork corrosion and concrete durability over the course of the coming millennium. Almost poignantly, the eco-friendly engineering firm Fulcrum Consulting puts a good spin on the implications of building a skyscraping Buddha in the middle of nowhere: "The lack of existing infrastructures gives us the

---

* Lama Yeshe's reincarnation was discovered in Spain a year after his death and is expected to pick up where the late lama left off when he completes his studies. This discovery was not difficult to make: the infant recognized as Lama Yeshe's reincarnation had recently been born to two of his students. Explaining the qualifications of the organization's once and future leader, the Maitreya Project's promotional materials explain, "His birth had been remarkably quick and painless, and he was very peaceful, never crying even when he was hungry."

opportunity to develop the Project sustainably from a 'clean slate.' This means we can start from scratch without the need to compromise designs in order to incorporate existing systems."

In addition to leading the project through its visionary to its practical phase, Lama Zopa also provided the endeavor with the stars of its traveling road show. He released the bulk of the relics for public display in 2001. By then the collection included not just the rainbow assortment of gemlike cremation stones that are the most common form of Buddhist relic, but an actual bone, a piece of shin that had once belonged— in the most personal sense—to the originator of the Maitreya Project himself, Lama Yeshe. Found among his ashes after he was cremated in 1984, the brown and yellow shard is the approximate size and shape of a sharpened pencil stub. Like a lot of relics, it has logged more miles dead than alive. As part of the living Lama Yeshe, the shinbone remained behind monastery walls for the better part of fifty years. As part of the Maitreya Project, the shinbone has visited forty countries on five continents, keeping up a schedule of nonstop travel since 2001.

While Lama Yeshe's leg and the other relics have been successful in raising awareness of the project and filling donation boxes, the promotional literature explains that a major Buddha statue naturally needs some major donors. In the tradition of stained-glass church windows and synagogue Torah arks, every part of the Maitreya Buddha statue is available as a named gift opportunity. Sponsorship of the head will cost you $25 million. The hands go for $6.5 million each, and the feet $5.5 million. You could also sponsor a few of the inch-tall figurines that will watch over the One Million Buddhas Shrine Room for a suggested donation of $100 each.

Whether this is an elaborate spiritual scam is perhaps too cynical a question. After all, Buddhism is a faith less of theory than of action. It invites its devotees, metaphorically, to lay their money down. It's a gamble. You won't know before you're dead if you've lived the kind of virtuous life that creates gleaming relics of human remains, so until then you should put your karma where your mouth is. If the stakes are too high to buy in for a hundred-dollar donation, there are penny antes to be had: a single square inch of one of the five thousand brass-plated panels that will cover the statue from toe to crown will run you just ten bucks.

That seems to be the most popular size of donation at the relic tour's stop at Golden Bridge. When I ask the yoga practitioners and other relic enthusiasts waiting in line what has brought them here, very few know much or care about the statue being built half a world away. As far as the yoga people are concerned, they have purchased the relics themselves for a few hours. The point of the whole enterprise matters far less than how the relics make them feel. Though they might have come looking for something "real," they leave satisfied with feeling, as I am told more than once, "really, really good."

✳

AT GOLDEN BRIDGE that night, after the Heart Shrine Relic Tour's visit to Hollywood has come to an end, I join the custodian of the relics and a handful of helpful yoga students repacking the relic van with its treasures.

Carmen Straight and I carry the scale model of the world's biggest Buddha by his child-sized legs and load him into the passenger seat, strapping a shoulder belt across his chest.

"This is how he rides when we fly," Carmen tells me.

And the relics? I wonder. Were priceless pieces of Lama Yeshe and other Buddhist sages being entrusted to baggage handlers, cargo holds, and the possibilities of lost luggage?

"Oh, no. I keep them in a carry-on," Carmen says. "They're more comfortable that way."

I am about to bid Carmen and I Fung farewell when they inform me that before leaving town the relics have one more stop. Among those feeling "really, really good," at least if such reactions can be judged by panting, howling, and wagging of tails, were the nonhuman recipients of the relics' blessings. Pets were welcome throughout the Golden Bridge exhibition and Carmen Straight had not hesitated when it came time to lower the Buddha reliquary onto furry heads and wet noses. The dogs didn't seem to mind, but at least one cat reacted to the blessing as if it were a bath, which spiritually speaking might not be so far off.

The most ardent animal lover to visit the relic tour in Hollywood was a bearded sprite of a fellow named Allan Mootnick. He was so touched by his visit to the relics and the power he felt among them that he returned to invite Carmen to bring the relics to meet and bless some friends of his.

"We'll be here all weekend," Carmen told him. "Maybe they could come to us?"

"They'd love to," Mootnick said, "but I can't let them out of their cages."

Mootnick had a gibbon reservation on the desert edge of the city. In his travels as a primatologist he had visited many Buddhist countries, he explained. Wherever he went, he tried to bring back two things: a specimen of the local gibbon species and a Buddha statue; more than once he flew back from Asia with Buddhas in his luggage and gibbons in live cargo crates.

With all his Buddhas and gibbons now gathered in one place not far from Golden Bridge, he loved the idea of the relics coming out there as well. Carmen said the relic tour really ought to be moving on, but to her it seemed the relics wanted to go. "All these things are from Buddhist lands, it will be like a reunion," she said.

Bright and early the next morning, I travel with Carmen, I Fung, and a van full of relics out of Los Angeles and into the desert.

We pull up to a chain-link, canvas, and concrete compound that looks like a set from *Mad Max* and are uncertain we have found the right place until we open the windows. Gibbons yelp and scream like playground children who've enjoyed a snack of too much chocolate only to be chased by a pack of dogs. The gibbons rattle cages and clang pots and pans and unleash long strings of yelping—"Woop! Woop! Woop! Woop!"

Mootnick meets us at the gate and unlocks a series of chains designed to keep the gibbons in and the people out. The moment we're inside the enclosure the screeching goes from loud to cataclysmic—"Woop! Woop! Woop! Woop!"— like an entire parking garage full of the noisiest car alarms you can imagine.

"So you brought the relics?" Mootnick asks.

Carmen nods as she displays a specially designed travel case of quilted fabric in six or seven vibrant colors—a relic cozy. She explains that the case holds selected relics for the occasion and that she would be doing a "walking blessing" in order "to let all of the animals share in the benefit."

As we walk, Mootnick keeps up a running commentary on how he thought the gibbons were reacting to the blessing and to the presence of the relics generally. Roughly every other word is interrupted by the almost psychotic screaming of the creatures in their cages.

"When you think about it . . ." Mootnick says.

"Woop! Woop! Woop!" the gibbons reply.

"Both the primates and the relics are all from Buddhist . . ."

"Ayayayaya!"

"Lands. So there must be some . . ."

"Baa-waa-waa-waa-WOOP!"

"Affinity between them."

"Could be," Carmen says.

"*Achiachiachiachi!*"

"Oh, they are definitely changing their calls," Mootnick says. "Listen to that."

Those of us who have never heard the madness of gibbons in conversation can only take his word for it.

"So they are usually not as loud?" Carmen asks.

"Oh, usually they're much louder. The relics must be calming them."

They throw themselves off walls, swing on ropes, and

fling themselves from one end of the cages to the other. Finally, we get to an enclosure that is completely silent.

"This one seems to know the relics are here," Carmen says.

"Actually," Mootnick says, "I think this one is just upset that there is a new adult male nearby." He shoots an accusing glare my way. "They're very territorial. He looks at you and sees competition for mates. That makes him angry. If we get any closer, watch out."

"You don't think the relics would calm him?" I ask.

"Don't bet on it," he says.

3

ONE, TWO, THREE, FORESKIN

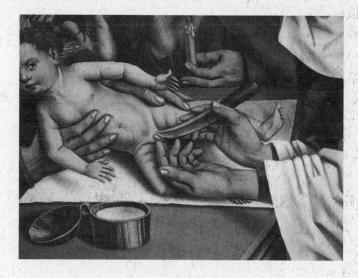

GO LOOKING FOR RELICS AND YOU WON'T ALWAYS FIND them—I've found some shrines closed for renovations, some lost to history, others blocked by armed guards—but people with relics on the brain are often closer than you'd think.

At least it seems so at the moment. I am riding in the backseat of a car-service Lincoln on my way to yet another airport, this time in New York, when the driver turns his head to the side to make the strangest attempt at small talk I've ever heard.

"So," he says, "what do you think about Jesus's bones?"

He's wearing one of those cell phone earpieces and shouting toward the windshield, so at first I can't tell if he is talking to me. It seems just as likely he's having an early morning discussion about first-century archaeology with his dispatcher or his wife. Then he catches my eye in the rearview mirror.

"They found them," he says. "You heard, right?"

The newspaper beside him tells the tale. He is talking about a recent announcement that Israeli archaeologist Simcha Jacobovici claimed to have found a particularly controversial grave site in Jerusalem. The filmmaker James Cameron had made a documentary about it, and so the news was getting, yes, *Titanic* attention. Cruising along at seventy miles an hour, weaving in and out of traffic on a swerving stretch of highway, I wonder if it was worth mentioning that, in fact, the archaeologist had not found actual bones, just ossuaries, "bone boxes," or that scholars the world over raised a collective eyebrow at the possibility of the boxes having once contained the remains of Jesus and his family.

The driver seems a true believer on the subject, however, and I don't want to upset him. As we squeeze between a tractor trailer and a concrete highway divider, I worry if voicing my doubts about Jesus's tomb would increase the likelihood that my own "bone box" might turn out to be a charcoal gray town car with leather seats.

I don't need to say anything. It soon becomes clear that— to the driver, at least—what has actually been found in the dirt of the Holy City is beside the point.

As he speeds up and I strap on my seat belt, he explains his interest in Jesus's bones by telling a story of lapsed church attendance but lingering faith. He tells me how he and his wife decide how much money to spend on Christmas then give half to the soup kitchen instead. ("Our own meal just tastes better that way," he says.) Then he tells me that he knows a guy who used to have one leg shorter than the other, but a miracle lady touched him and made him whole.

"No kidding, buddy. I saw it," he says. "His leg grew an inch and a half."

We're at a stoplight in front of hospital called Mercy—a coincidence so perfect it gives me a surreal and disoriented feeling—when he turns around and tells me, "Then the miracle lady touched my bad knee." He stares hard at me through tinted lenses. "And I was healed, too."

When the light changes, he turns to get back to driving, now with a little less intensity. He seems transported by the memory. He even repeats his point, as if to no one, "My knee, I swear. *Healed*."

That's when it hits me. We aren't talking about Jesus's bones anymore. We're talking about *his* bones. We aren't talking about a documentary and the deaths it purports to prove. We're talking about one man and the people he cares about, the kind of life he tries to live.

Is this why I was traveling the world looking at relics? It's certainly part of it. Like the long-ago occupants of bone boxes dug up in Jerusalem, and like any saint of whom only a scrap remains, the spiritual lives of others can be known only through glimpses and guesses. Faith makes everyone a mystery, and stories about faith can sometimes remind us how little we know about one another.

After a few minutes in the slow lane, my driver returns from his spiritual reverie. He drives the rest of the trip hard and fast. Gripping the hand rest in the backseat, I ask him again about his story. Did a miracle lady really heal him?

"Yeah, but you know I had two bad knees and she only fixed one," he says. "But that's another story."

✳

FOR A PLACE so full of history, faith, and death, Jerusalem has fewer relics than you might expect. It is a city of profound absences: nearly everything that once made it holy is either gone or, having been demolished, exists now only as a reconstructed shadow of its former self.

Today the city's most popular spiritual attractions are

visited precisely because of what is no longer there: the Western Wall commemorates Judaism's twice destroyed Temple; the Dome of the Rock mosque is the site of Muhammad's flight from the earth—the "rock" in question is where he stepped to mount his winged horse; and the Church of the Holy Sepulchre is uniquely famous as a tomb vacant for roughly 715,819 days and occupied for only three. Once the world capital of relics, Jerusalem now lags well behind Rome, and even Pittsburgh.*

The Crusades are partially responsible for this. Every time European Christians got it in their heads that they should reclaim the Holy Land, what many of them really had in mind was a reclamation of the fortunes they imagined had been stockpiled there. After laying siege to the infidel lands where the origins of their faith might be found, armies of pious treasure hunters left blue-eyed Arab children behind and brought back as many keepsakes as they could carry. Between the tenth and thirteenth centuries, the True Cross (which certainly wasn't), the Spear of Destiny (destined to turn up in at least a dozen places through the years), and a few of the many heads of John the Baptist all disappeared from the churches of Jerusalem.

Such relics of the Holy Land were especially prized because the moment each became an object of religious

---

* To be fair, every city besides Rome currently lags behind Pittsburgh in its relic population. Saint Anthony's Chapel, in the Troy Hill section of Pittsburgh, claims to be second only to the Vatican in its collection. Founded by a nineteenth-century priest who scoured Europe buying up pieces of saints he found in pawnshops, it boasts upwards of five thousand relics.

significance is recorded so clearly in scripture. The True Cross upon which Jesus was crucified is, of course, crucial in all four Gospels; the Spear of Destiny, used by a Roman soldier to stab him as he died, is mentioned in the Gospel of John; and the moment John the Baptist's head left his body, and thus became a relic, appears in Matthew, Mark, and Luke. According to the Gospel accounts, Salome, the daughter of Galilee ruler Herod, danced for her drunken father one night and so pleased him that he promised her anything she desired. When she asked for the Baptist's head and reminded Herod that he had given his word, he had no choice but to oblige. It's easy to imagine the draw that such a story—at once sexy, bloody, and duty-bound—would have on your average Crusader. The desire to find John the Baptist's head in Jerusalem was so fervent that at least four of them made their way back to Europe.

Perhaps because of the contemporary conflation some pundits and politicians make between the Crusades of old and the wars of today, it is easy to suppose that the European incursions into the lands we now call the Middle East were fought in the name of spreading a particular belief system or way of life. It is not the case, however, that the kings and popes responsible wished to go to war with Islam, or even with infidels broadly defined. Such modern connections obscure the extent to which the Crusades were fought for relics. By any historian's reckoning, the Crusades are considered among the defining events of the past millennium or so; they would have been unimaginable if not for the hold relics once held on the collective imagination of Christendom.

Jerusalem itself was considered one big reliquary. It gained this reputation with the help of the mother of the first Christian ruler of the Roman Empire. Constantine's mother, Helen, came to the Holy Land in the fourth century for the same reason Crusaders would follow her trail six hundred years later: to fill her pockets with as much holy loot as she could carry. Among her first and most important finds was supposedly a cave containing three ancient crosses, which local tradition held were the implements of death for Jesus and the two thieves crucified alongside him. Finding three crosses would have created a conundrum. Three identical items, and yet only one could be considered holy. Which of these things was not like the other?

To solve this problem, Helen directed a sick woman who had been traveling with her party to lie atop the crosses one after the other, Goldilocks style. After the first two crosses she remained sick, but the third was apparently just right. She was healed of her illness, and thus Helen knew which of the crosses had been used for the only crucifixion that mattered.

Needless to say, this cross did not remain in Jerusalem. It was among the first of countless sacred objects that would be exported to the far corners of the empire. It didn't take long for the locals to realize they had little hope of keeping the most sought-after relics in the city, and so they soon began playing along. By the time King Louis IX of France got involved in the relic hunt, King Baldwin II, the ruler of the Knights Templar who governed Jerusalem from 1118 to 1131, gladly served as broker for the French sovereign's purchase of both the Crown of Thorns and another head of John the Baptist.

And it was not just kings who hoped to acquire relics during the Crusades. The vast majority of those who undertook these armed pilgrimages were poor and became only more abused and abject during the course of the arduous journey. They wanted not only the spiritual benefits a crusade offered—indulgences that promised sinners time off from purgatory—but the financial rewards as well. Whether intended as donations to the church back home or items to be sold at the first opportunity, relics were both the motivation for joining the righteous armies heading south and, if one was lucky enough to acquire them, proof that the pilgrimage had been undertaken. It was often said during the Middle Ages that many a poor man had been made rich by Jerusalem.

So much was to be gained through the accumulation of relics that the original market could not provide supply to meet the demand. After twice conquering Jerusalem and picking it clean of its religious treasures, the Crusaders deemed the relic well of the Holy City to be dry. It wasn't hard to find other sources. At the time, Constantinople—thanks in large part to Constantine's mother—had the largest collection of relics and saints' graves in the world. Then the seat of the Byzantine Church, which would later call itself Orthodox, it had been the Rome of the East for two centuries, since the schism between the Western and Eastern wings of the faith had torn Christendom in two.

The raiders from the Christian West pillaged the holiest

city of the Christian East in 1204, taking artifacts, including another piece of John the Baptist (his left forearm); the foot of Saint Cosmas; much of the True Cross; hairs from Jesus's beard; the skull of Saint Stephen, the first Christian martyr; and the finger that Saint Thomas (the famous doubter) stuck into Jesus's wound post-resurrection for proof that it was real. The most painful loss to many was the headless body of Saint John Chrysostom. A fourth-century archbishop whose talent for preaching gave him the name "Golden Mouth," Chrysostom was apparently as stubborn in death as he was eloquent in life. His body, it was said, could not be moved without permission from the deceased himself. Even when the emperor Theodosius tried to transfer the body in AD 438, the sarcophagus in which Chrysostom rested would not be moved. The emperor sat down and wrote a letter to the saint:

"Holy Father, It was only because we thought that your body is dead like the bodies of others are dead that we tried to move you. We only wanted to transfer it close to us. You who has taught repentance for all, forgive us. Remit yourself to us as a present, like a father to his children who love him, and give us joy with your presence."

Only when this letter was placed atop the coffin did the corpse of Chrysostom allow itself to be relocated. When the Western crusaders snatched it up without so much as a "please," it seemed to refute centuries of Eastern religious tradition.

In recent years, the Vatican has given key relics back to the Orthodox Church in an effort to heal an eight-hundred-year-old wound. In one of his last major acts as pope, John

Paul II returned Chrysostom's body to the Orthodox Patri-
archate. "In the transferal of such holy relics," he wrote to
the patriarch of Constantinople, "we find a blessed occasion
to purify our wounded memories in order to strengthen our
journey of reconciliation."

Considering that hundreds of saints were taken from
Constantinople to Rome, the Orthodox might have been for-
given for saying these reparations were too little too late. Yet
the gesture won the Orthodox over. Between the lines of the
pope's letter was an echo of the letter written to Chrysostom
himself long before. "Sorry," the pope seemed to be saying,
"we shouldn't have moved your bones."

✳

NO PLANS HAVE been made to give relics back to Jerusalem,
and so at least as far as objects of Christian veneration go, the
city remains something of an empty tomb.

Nonetheless, one goes to Jerusalem hoping to see something particularly holy, especially when one arrives during a
season of claims made concerning Jesus's bones. It was not
just James Cameron and Simcha Jacobovici making declara-
tions of discovery. In the wake of the bone-box announcement, a small news item had rippled briefly across the media
as a footnote to the more widely publicized story.

"Christian researchers," the report said, "are excavating a
site in the Mount of Olives Cemetery outside the walls of
Jerusalem which may hold clues to some of the burials of Jesus's disciples."

According to the Israel-based journalist who penned the

piece, Mitch Ugana, the researchers' findings had been written up in a periodical called the *Judaistic Review*.

"When they carefully moved the olive tree," Mitch Ugana wrote, "they found a white cross with the Greek inscription 'To the God Jesus Christos.'" He also suggested that there was a "far-fetched possibility that the discovery is the site of the 'Holy Prepuce,' an allusion to the historical belief that Mary, according to Jewish custom, buried the prepuce (the 'remnants' taken after a circumcision) of Jesus."

The story of a relic's appearance in modern-day Jerusalem was certainly intriguing, especially a relic with such a long history of disappearances as this one. The Holy Prepuce, the foreskin of Jesus Christ, is perhaps the most famous missing relic in the world. It is generally believed that the prepuce was last seen in 1983, in a little hill town of Calcata, Italy, where thieves broke into a church and made off with its jewel-encrusted reliquary. A great loss to the locals, no doubt, but the Roman Catholic Church as a whole was not entirely sorry to see it go. And, in any event, they had reason to take it in stride: before this most recent disappearance, it had gone missing as often as it appeared.

✳

THEFT HAS BEEN as much a part of the tradition of relics as veneration has. As described in exhaustive detail by Patrick Geary's *Furta Sacra: Thefts of Relics in the Central Middle Ages*, relic theft once played a social role more complex than simply filling a burglar's pockets with ill-gotten gain. Geary should know: a professor of history at UCLA, his other works include *Living with the Dead in the Middle Ages* and such landmark scholarly articles in the study of relics as "The Humiliation of the Saints."*

As objects of unparalleled worth, relics were a form of extraordinary currency. In addition to being plundered as they were during the Crusades, they were given as gifts, offered as dowries, and traded for prestige, influence, and access. For a period of centuries—much longer than the American dollar has been worth the paper it's printed on—relics were the true coin of the realm.

At first, it was only the rich or the ecclesiastically well connected who made use of relic "dealers," as thieves preferred to be known. Later, as the desire for relics trickled down into the medieval version of the middle class, anyone might buy a relic or two. At every level, it was a business. There were, of course, amateurs, such as the zealous Portuguese lady who bit off Saint Francis Xavier's toes, but there were also those far more pragmatic in their relic acquisition—"professionals," as Geary calls them.

"Relic thieves operated much like other types of merchants," he writes. Some "organized periodic caravans, which

---

* The Humiliation of the Saints was more or less what it sounds like. When things went well for a medieval monastery, the monks naturally praised and thanked the saints whose relics they possessed for their good fortune. When things weren't going so well, the monks did not live by that addendum to the golden rule: if you don't have anything nice to say, don't say anything at all. Geary shows that Christian monastics of the eleventh century regularly took part in ritual insulting and cursing of the relics in their care; the monks would take the relics out of their cases, put them on the ground, and do their best, through subtly altered tones in their recitation of the day's prayers, to insult and "punish" the saints.

crossed the Alps in spring and made the rounds of monastic fairs." Most dealers "dealt in a wide variety of merchandise and simply added relics to their wares whenever the opportunity arose."

In a three-year span of the 830s, the most intrepid of relic merchants, Deusdona—whose name in Latin means, appropriately enough, "God giver"—stole and successfully sold pieces of saints both famous and obscure, including Alexandrus, Castulus, Concordia, Emerentiana, Favianus, Felicissimus, Felicitas, Maurus, Pamphilus, Papia, Sebastian, Urbanus, and Victoria. Much of the Eternal City had been built atop a vast necropolis. Deusdona, who possessed an encyclopedic knowledge of the graves of Rome, harvested as if it were his private vegetable garden. Then off he went with his crops, as if to a farmers' market on a summer day.

"From the merchants' point of view, relics were excellent articles of trade," Geary continues. "They were small and easily transported, since entire bodies of saints centuries dead were nothing more than dust and a few bones that could be carried in a small bag. As highly desirable luxury items, they brought excellent return for little capital investment." Of course, sometimes they required no investment at all. Wherever relic merchants traveled to sell their wares, new bodies—some holy, some not—were in great supply.

As any good relic merchant or used-car salesman could insist, it was not only the seller who benefited. A stolen relic gave a community a certain cachet, whether it was a monastery, a convent, or the town surrounding a church. There was much to be gained by creating the impression that faith there was so powerful that relics would be obtained by any means necessary. One French monastery went so far as to change its name to let the world know it had increased the contents of its relic treasury. With a new moniker, Charroux—meaning "red flesh"—it grew to be one of the most significant monastic houses in Europe.

There was even a literature devoted to claims of how and when a relic was stolen. The formal term for the movement of a relic from one church to another was translation—from the Latin "to carry over," just as we now do with languages. *Translationes,* then, were a genre of medieval letters that recounted the removal of relics from one site and their delivery to another. Even when a relic was acquired through perfectly legitimate means, a story might be concocted to give the bones in question a whiff not of death, which they had already, but of piety so great it was willing to brave any danger. And naturally, wherever a relic turned up was deemed the place God had intended.

History tends to look unfavorably on theft. Even Geary, who is mostly sympathetic of relic thieves, cannot help but include a harsh verdict: "At best the thieves were high class fences, at worst grave robbers." But they were also like brokers or commodities traders. They provided a valuable service by moving assets from one hand to another—sometimes against the wishes of the first hand, but no one said business was easy. In any event, the rewards outweighed the risks, not least of all because the commodities in question could be produced with little more than a shovel and a map to the graveyards of Rome.

"The best aspect of all," Geary notes, "owing to the difficulties of communication between communities involved, was that the body of a popular saint already sold might be sold again to another customer."

Perhaps the most intriguing part of the relic-based economy that thrived for so long in the Middle Ages is that, officially speaking, trading in relics is strictly forbidden within the Christian tradition. The offense even has its own name: *simony,* the buying and selling of sacred objects and offices.

The word comes from a scene in the Acts of the Apostles when a false miracle worker called Simon Magus sees the followers of Jesus passing along the power of the Holy Spirit through the laying on of hands. Simon Magus offers the apostle Peter money and begs him, "Give me also this power, that on whomsoever I lay hands, he may receive it." Peter's reply—"Thy money perish with thee, because thou hast thought that the gift of God may be purchased"—established the church's official position on the market in spiritual goods.

Early on, simony had nothing to do with relics but with the sale of sacraments, the seven officially sanctioned, and ecclesiastically controlled, blessings of the Catholic Church. During the eras when membership in the priesthood was regarded as the key to a life of leisure, ordination was the most common sacrament offered for sale. So pervasive was the practice, it was outlawed three times, first in 451, at the Council of Chalcedon, then in 1179, at the Third Lateran Council, and again in 1545 at the Council of Trent. As relic possession became as desirable as the priesthood, the charge of simony began to be leveled against bone dealers as well.

Church law states plainly, "It is strictly forbidden to sell sacred relics," but there is, fortunately for merchants, a loophole. While relics cannot be bought or sold, they can be given as donations, and donations can be given in return. Restrictions on simony thus had an unexpected effect on the relic market. As any clerk in a fancy boutique will tell you, the ones without the price tag are the most expensive of all.

✳

THE QUESTION OF what relics are really worth is at the forefront of my mind as I land in Jerusalem and try to get my bearings. I have only a printout of Mitch Ugana's short news item to guide me as I attempt to track down any trace of the divine prepuce that might be found in the Holy Land. The one landmark mentioned in the story, the Mount of Olives Cemetery, should be easy enough to find. Tradition holds that it is close to the site of the Garden of Gethsemane, where Jesus prayed the night before his crucifixion. It's on the far side of the Old City from where I am staying with a friend, and so my first trek in that direction sends me through the heart of the holiest and bloodiest .35 square miles in the world.

It is common in Jerusalem to get lost while attempting to walk the straightest possible line from point A to point B. It is less common that one lost on the twisting streets will be led directly to the Church of the Holy Sepulchre. This might have something to do with my tendency to follow mobs of singing pilgrims whenever they cross my path. When looking for relics, a mob of pilgrims is a sensible star to travel by.

As it turns out, the Holy Sepulchre itself has much to do with the Christian tradition of relic theft. Legend has it that the church was founded during the same fourth-century trip made by Constantine's mother, Helen. She sent most of the treasures she gathered home to Constantinople. The rest she kept here, her own personal relic warehouse.

The church remains full of loot, but none of it is of the bodily variety. This is not to say things do not occasionally get physical within these walls. Like Jerusalem itself, the Holy Sepulchre is uneasily divided and endlessly contested. Its very structure suggests a collaboration between feuding architects: in one section a glass door leads to a modern chapel decorated with twentieth-century metal sculpture lit by electric gallery bulbs; in another, heavy dark wood and stone are stained black by sixteen centuries of candlelight. Shared equally by monks of Catholic, Orthodox, and Armenian persuasions, the church in modern times has been the scene of frequent squabbles and fistfights—even all-out brawls—over who owns what within the consecrated space.

These tensions make sense when considering the whole place is basically a walk-in relic; every nook and cranny of it was purportedly touched by Jesus, either in his last moments or when he was laid in the tomb. The site of the crucifixion, called Golgotha, "the place of the skull," is inside the entrance to the right, up a set of stone stairs that gets clogged with believers just before noon; it seems every guide in the city likes to end his morning tour on a high note before setting his charges free for lunch. The tomb—the Holy Sepulchre itself—is about twenty yards away.

The proximity of the place of the crucifixion to the place of burial is entirely unbiblical and ahistorical, but no one seems to mind. I wander the church's cavernous chapels and passageways until I have convinced myself there are indeed no bodily relics to be found here. Then I find a place to sit and reread Mitch Ugana's prepuce story, studying it like a map to buried treasure. It seems I am sitting a bit too close to the Orthodox section of the church, because a dour-looking monk in yards of black cloth keeps eyeing me, sizing me up. Perhaps I do not look sufficiently Orthodox to him, and my chosen seat in his quadrant is bringing his blood to a boil.

No matter. I refocus on Mitch Ugana's words. Had he been there when the archaeologists "carefully moved the olive tree"? I wonder. What had he seen that led to the mention of the Jewish tradition of burying the remnant taken after circumcision?

A cloud of dark fabric brushes by me, and I brace for a scolding. When I look up, however, it is not a gruff monk come to escort me from the Orthodox section but three Muslim women hurrying by. All three wear full-length abayas that only occasionally show flashes of sneakers as they move quickly across the floor. It is impossible to tell the ages of the two whose faces are fully covered, but the third wears a veil pulled open around her cheeks, framing her face. She seems to be about twenty, but the way the three of them run together arm in arm they could easily still be in their teens.

Fascinated, I watch them as they pose for pictures. They

trade turns, so that every third photo finds the one whose face is visible taking pictures of the two whose faces are hidden.

The revealed one catches me staring. When she does not look away, I hold both hands in front of my face, making a slight clicking motion with my right index finger, presenting, I hope, a universal sign that says, "Would you like me to take a picture?"

The girls look at one another, then at me, then at one another. The uncovered one nods excitedly as she hands me their camera. I take their picture as they stand at the foot of the stairs that lead to Golgotha.

The two fully covered women climb the stairs first, leaving the less covered one standing alone for the first time since they entered the church. Perhaps because her more modest friends have for a moment wandered away, she gets bold, apparently deciding that standing with a complete stranger at the foot of the hill where Christ was crucified is an excellent opportunity to try out her English.

"What has brought you to Jerusalem?" she asks haltingly.

"I'm here looking for something," I say.

She looks left, she looks right. Coast is clear.

"I am looking also."

Most likely she has taken my answer to mean that I am simply seeing the sites, as she is; but I imagine I detect something conspiratorial in her tone, as if we're in this together.

In either case, I am fairly certain we are not looking for the same thing. She rushes off before I can ask.

✳

THAT NO ONE knows what happened to Jesus's foreskin is particularly interesting because there used to be upwards of a dozen in circulation. Churches and monasteries throughout Europe—in France, Italy, Germany, Belgium, and Spain—all claimed to have one at various times, never mind that each knew full well about the claims of the others. Some medieval commentators went so far as to suggest that the tiny slip of skin multiplied itself—through budding, perhaps, or maybe through some other kind of cellular reproduction more in keeping with its pink and wormy appearance. Others speculated that no replication was necessary; there could easily be numerous authentic relics of the foreskin if the pieces were cut small enough.

Advocates of either the multiplication or the division hypothesis would have found support in the fact that from the earliest days in Christian tradition there seemed to be at least two foreskins making the rounds.

One was accounted for by Saint Birgitta of Sweden, who in her popular *Revelations* said it was worn by the Virgin Mary as jewelry all the days of her life. The Virgin Mary told Birgitta this herself in a vision. Before her ascension to heaven, she explained, she took her murdered son's foreskin from her neck and presented it to Saint John the Evangelist, who in turn passed it along to his community of disciples.

Assuming Jesus's mohel didn't make any extra cuts, the other tale of the foreskin's origins directly contradicts Birgitta's story. This one comes from an older source, the apocryphal Gospel of Thomas, which is concerned mainly with Christ's earliest days.

And when the time of his circumcision was come, namely, the eighth day, on which the law commanded the child to be circumcised, they circumcised him in a cave.

And the old Hebrew woman took the foreskin (others say she took the navel-string), and preserved it in an alabaster-box of oil of spikenard.

And she had a son who was a druggist, to whom she said, "Take heed thou sell not this alabaster box of spikenard-ointment, although thou shouldst be offered three hundred pence for it."

You'd think the druggist would listen to his mother, good Jewish boy that he was. Yet, as the Gospel goes on to explain, the ointment box and the foreskin it contained were later sold to none other than Mary Magdalene. Some may doubt this story not only because of the astonishing circular coincidence, but also because of where it appears. The Gospel of Thomas is one of the many texts written by early followers of Jesus that for a variety of reasons—questionable reliability among them—did not make it into the mainstream of Christian literature. Yet the ointment mentioned above makes an appearance in other Gospels as well. According to canonical texts (that is, those stories included in the New Testament as it appears in most Bibles), some thirty-three years after the circumcision, Mary Magdalene purchased oil with which to anoint Jesus. If the apocryphal sources are to be believed, she made this purchase in the shop of the very man who had been entrusted with a little piece of the savior all those years before. Whether or not she noticed something floating in the ointment when she bought it, neither the apocryphal nor the canonical Gospels say.

In any event, it is through one of these two provenances that the various sacred foreskins were thought to have been preserved for posterity. After that, they did a remarkable job lying low. Even as the mania for relics developed and spread from Polycarp's Smyrna to every corner of Christendom, not a peep was heard about the Holy Prepuce for roughly the next seven and a half centuries. The first known historical mention of the relic came in the year 800, when the Holy Roman Emperor Charlemagne gave it as a gift to Pope Leo II.

At this point the story multiplies again, for three rival legends explain how the relic came into Charlemagne's possession in the first place. The story Charlemagne himself liked to tell was that during a visit to Jerusalem, a chorus of angels greeted him in the Holy Sepulchre and personally bestowed upon him the most precious ounce of human skin in the world. He likely favored this story because the less miraculous explanation raised questions he would have preferred to avoid. The foreskin was more likely a coronation gift from Irene of Athens, empress of Byzantium. She wasn't just being friendly. As a female ruler in a very male world, she hoped to shore up her power through a marriage to Charlemagne. Perhaps a severed piece of penis had a different cultural significance in AD 800, but in modern experience it seems an odd engagement present. Charlemagne refused the offer but kept the gift.

Given the distance between the miracle of one explanation and the prosaic, even sordid, nature of the other, it's no surprise that some sought a middle ground. How did Charlemagne acquire the foreskin? One day a mysterious man wandered into the cathedral the emperor had built and gave it to him, simple as that. The package delivered was a leather pouch containing the last earthly evidence of the Son of God. According to scholarship the history of the prepuce has generated, the leather purse in which Charlemagne received the relic not only bore a striking resemblance to a scrotum, it became the inspiration for fashions of the day. The flouncy bulbous sleeves of the French aristocracy may seem feminine to modern eyes, but back in the day they had the exact opposite meaning. They signaled manliness in an obvious way.

However the foreskins of Jesus entered the territory and imagination of Christian Europe, they instantly became among the most popular and talked-about relics. They were, after all, the only physical, bodily connection to Jesus. To have them was to have a direct line to unquestionable authority and power. When Charlemagne made a gift of the prepuce to the pope, he was, in effect, letting the pontiff know who was in charge. If such a relic was his to give, so, too, was power.

As the prime architect of what would become Western Europe and thus a singular force of the Middle Ages, Charlemagne naturally had relics to spare. The Aachen Cathedral (in what is now Germany), where he reportedly received the prepuce, was already home to some of the most important relics of the day. Jesus's swaddling clothes, his loincloth, and his mother Mary's cloak were all kept in Aachen's treasury. Later,

Charlemagne himself would be added to the collection. He died in 814 and was entombed in the church he built. One hundred and eighty-six years after his entombment, his successor Otto III opened Charlemagne's crypt and found him sitting upright, with a Bible open in his lap. Charlemagne's body, Otto would later claim, was entirely intact, except for the nose, which had apparently fallen away. Legend has it that Otto reached into the dead man's mouth, pulled a tooth, and started to back out of the tomb. Then, as if stricken by the need to make a fair trade, he ordered a nose fashioned out of gold be affixed to Charlemagne's mostly incorrupt face. For a man who claimed ownership of the prepuce, an end more fraught with Freudian symbolism is difficult to imagine.

Others claimed a different kind of ownership. Saint Birgitta was just one of many medieval mystics—all nuns—who told of the foreskin appearing to them in visions. Some, most famously Saint Catherine of Siena, imagined wearing the foreskin as a wedding ring; others, such as Austrian mystic Agnes Blannbekin, ate it. These were merely visions, however. Given the foreskin's most sought-after miraculous property, it's no surprise church authorities would want to keep the relic out of nunnish hands. The foreskin held by the Benedictine monastery at Coulombs in France was sent to England in 1421 to be placed near Henry V's wedding bed. Apparently because of the circumstances of Christ's own conception it was thought the presence of the prepuce would ensure pregnancy. The sweet odor it emitted was said to make for an easy delivery nine months later. Many a queen made use of its powers.

Things got rough for the foreskins of Jesus as the Middle Ages matured. First, the prepuce claimed by the monastery at Charroux (such was the "red flesh" they were named for) was destroyed by the Huguenots in the religious wars that bloodied France. Then the Roman prepuce went missing when Charles V invaded the city in 1527. And these were nothing compared to the theological attacks it suffered. While the value of such an artifact was obvious to the common medieval believer, the idea of a piece of Jesus's "human fully, fully divine" flesh still lingering somewhere on earth posed a puzzle to the professionals. Christ was thought to reside in Heaven in the fullness of his perfection. If this was the case, how could he not have all the parts with which he was born? For Christians who believed the covenant displayed by the Jewish ritual of circumcision had been replaced by the covenant of baptism, it created a larger problem: did Jesus in heaven have a Jewish penis?

The answer implied by the survival of the foreskin was too much for many. The prepuce made some Christians so uneasy that it has been considered as the most Jewish of relics, and so should not be deemed appropriate for Christian worship. The fact that Judaism as a rule does not have relics mattered little. Within the spectrum of Christian artifacts, this tiny slip of skin served as a reminder of the tradition from which the savior, and thus the faith he inspired, had come.

Naturally this interpretation only intensified arguments about its substance and meaning. Some contended that the foreskin was not properly understood as skin at all, but rather as something like a fingernail or a hair clipping or excrement. It was natural for such things to be left behind by a fully human body, even if it was also fully divine, so really the foreskin posed no problem. Not so fast, others said. When Jesus ascended to heaven, anything he left on earth would have ascended with him, his foreskin flapping up to the clouds like a butterfly. This particular belief was given a scientific patina in the seventeenth century when Leo Allatius, a classicist and custodian of the Vatican Library, proposed that the prepuce had gone beyond the clouds and into space, not stopping (and expanding, apparently) until it reached Saturn, where it became the distant planet's then recently discovered ring.

No other foreskin could have caused such trouble. Because of the theological understandings regarding Jesus's body, any piece of it posed questions other relics did not. And because of Jesus's centrality to the faith, any piece of him was fraught with meaning and the potential for dispute. This made it a popular target when the tide turned against relics. Most of the foreskins were casualties of time and revolutions both religious and political, a sad end to a relic once so ubiquitous it prompted the great scourge of Rome, John Calvin, to wonder just how big the member of the Lord must have been if a dozen clippings could be taken without exhausting the supply.

By the twentieth century, the dozen or so pieces of the prepuce had been whittled down to four, three of which were located at the Basilica of Saint John Lateran in Rome, the Benedictine abbey of Charroux (they rediscovered theirs in the middle of the nineteenth century), and the Collegiate Church of Antwerp. Another church—this one in the hill town of Calcata, Italy—claimed to have the relic but not to have displayed it since the sixteenth century. When it at last opened up the gates to its inner sanctum and removed the relic for veneration, Calcata put on such a display that it became known as the site of the true foreskin.

Calcata's modern prominence as the home of the prepuce has also made it a place at which modern scorn has been directed. Its most precious object became a source of ironic religious pondering for James Joyce, who devotes a few paragraphs of *Ulysses* to unzipping the prepuce's meaning. Standing at a urinal with Leopold Bloom, Stephen Dedalus looks down at his circumcised friend's member and cannot help but think of

The problem of sacerdotal integrity of
Jesus circumcised . . . and the problem as to
whether the divine prepuce, the carnal bridal ring of the
holy Roman Catholic
Apostolic church, conserved in Calcata,
were deserving of simple hyperduly or of the fourth degree
latria accorded to the
abscission of such divine excrescences as
hair and toenails.

Here Joyce is talking a bit of ecclesiastical nonsense, spoofing the language of the church and its angels-on-a-pinhead distinctions. *Latria* is the name given to church devotions directed specifically to God or Jesus; *hyperduly* is a variant of *hyperdulia*, the term for devotions associated with the Virgin Mary. Joyce is perhaps also making the theological point that in Catholic dogma woman is treated as something shed from a man—à la Eve growing from Adam's rib—and so perhaps the foreskin is better thought of as part of the feminine aspect of God (Mary) than the masculine (Jesus). Just as likely, as in much of *Ulysses*, he is simply writing as if he was paid by the word.

According to Joyce scholars, he did his homework, relying particularly on *Die "hochheilige Vorhaut Christi," im Kult und in der Theologie der Papstkirche*, by German theologian Alphons Victor Müller. Among Müller's primary concerns, and one that apparently grabbed Joyce's imagination, was whether the foreskin is in any way present at the moment of transubstantiation, when in Catholic theology the communion wafer becomes the actual flesh of Christ.

Perhaps because it had caught the mischievous attention of such infamous apostates as Joyce, the church began to downplay the foreskin's importance, and even questioned the propriety of mentioning it at all. The 1960s brought a modernizing moment in the Catholic Church known as the Second Vatican Council, after which many of the beloved ancient practices of the faithful were declared to be "pious legend." The prepuce alone was singled out and dismissed as an "irreverent curiosity."

Although mention of the foreskin became a punishable offense in ecclesiastical circles, the celebrations in Calcata continued. Through stubbornness and its somewhat remote location, Calcata became the repository of all accumulated legend and interest concerning the relic. When the relic disappeared in 1983, conspiracy theorists suggested the Catholic Church itself had finally grown tired of the embarrassment, as if the faith founded on Jesus's birth and death could not deal with a remnant of skin snipped from the most delicate part of his manhood when he was still a boy. A far simpler explanation is, as in the earliest days of relic theft, finance outweighed faith. Taken by common thieves and not Vatican operatives, the bejeweled reliquary of the Calcata prepuce is suspected to be in a private collection, or trimmed of its riches and cast aside, as it perhaps should have been—and may have been—two thousand years ago.

✳

MY NEXT ATTEMPT to get myself to the Mount of Olives Cemetery is no more successful than the first. The friend I am staying with suggests the best way to get to the other side of the Old City is not to cut through the ancient labyrinth but to catch a bus. He informs me the line closest to his apartment runs through a section of town until recently called the Valley of Death because of the number of suicide bombings it had seen. But don't worry, he tells me, these days everything is fine.

Undaunted, I march out from his apartment and climb aboard the first bus that stops. Once again I pore over my news clipping about the possible discovery of the prepuce, which I've now supplemented with a small file on the recent history of others who have attempted to recover it.

Ten years after the theft in Calcata, the British humorist and television personality Miles Kington traveled to Italy to locate the foreskin for the BBC. He didn't find it. In recent years, the American travel writer David Farley set off on a similar journey, with identical results. Calcata itself has become something of a hippie haven, drawing scores of artists and eccentrics, not a few of whom have had the same idea: finding the foreskin might be a way of going down in history and tweaking a stodgy old religion at the same time.

Riding through the Valley of Death on a sweltering summer day, I could not help but think such recent failures to recover the foreskin only supported the "far-fetched possibility" suggested by Mitch Ugana. Maybe the Calcata curiosity seekers were looking in the wrong place. Moreover, maybe it wasn't just them looking in the wrong place, but all of Christendom. For all the attention paid to the Italian prepuce, was it possible that the relic stolen twenty-five years ago was not the original foreskin? Given the work of relic dealers in the medieval period, it certainly seemed so. The nature of relics made it possible that even when you think you have one— even when you have one a dozen times over—you may never really have it all.

I'm miles from the Old City before I realize I've caught the wrong bus. The driver informs me that, in fact, I am well on my way to Mount Herzl, about as far from the ancient walled city as one can be while still in Jerusalem. Is there anything to see out there? I wonder. He points to a sign in Hebrew and English: "Yad Vashem."

Judaism does not have relics, but perhaps more than any other religion it does make a holy thing of memory, and it has objects that take on a spiritual intensity to rival anything displayed in a reliquary.

It is the middle of the day when the bus deposits me as close as it runs to the entrance of Israel's national Holocaust Memorial Museum. I walk a mile from the road alongside a half dozen boyish Israeli army soldiers with automatic rifles propped lazily over their shoulders like baseball bats. My shirt is soaked through with sweat before I arrive.

Much as I had in the Holy Sepulchre the day before, I wander and look and think in a place I had not intended to visit until my mind and heart can take no more. I see piles of shoes, walls made of pictures, of faces. Suddenly my concern for the prepuce, that supposedly most Jewish of relics, seems deeply and embarrassingly silly, if not perverse. The most Jewish of modern relics are, in fact, all around me. There are no bodies, of course; all the bodies have been lost.

Just then I look down into a display case and see two blond and perfect braids. When I read a placard beside the case I learn it is the hair of a little girl named Lili Hirsch. Before being sent to the camps her mother cut off Lili's braids and placed them inside a velvet bag usually used to hold a tallith, a prayer shawl.

"Forced to leave their home, Lili's mother Rivka knew she would not be able to care for her daughter's hair," the exhibit text says. "Chopping off Lili's two long braids, she promised they would be given to neighbors for safekeeping. Within six weeks Lili and her mother were murdered in Auschwitz."

Every relic is a stolen relic, I realize. Not only has it likely been stolen at least once in its storied history, it was also stolen, first, from the life of which it was a part.

✳

ON MY LAST day in Jerusalem I finally find it. Nestled on an incline sloping down toward the base of the hill that gives the walled Old City its commanding spot on the landscape, the Mount of Olives Cemetery has been a place of Jewish burial since biblical times. It is home to more than one hundred thousand graves; most of its natural features have been replaced by tombstones and rocky soil. The whole place has the dusty feel of an archaeological site, like a scar cut in the earth, but still I look everywhere for a sign of recent excavation.

As I wander among the graves, the details of the story I have been carrying around Jerusalem for days begin to pile up in my brain. "As they carefully moved the olive tree," Mitch Ugana had written. Surveying the rough terrain around me, any olive trees that gave the mount its name now seem long gone. ". . . they discovered a small white cross." A cross? How on earth could a relic of Jesus taken at the time of his birth be buried under the sign of his crucifixion? And where was it he said these findings had first been reported? The *Judaistic Review*? Is *Judaistic* even a word?

The ground grows hotter with every step, the air thicker, until it is almost impossible to breathe. "Where is it Mitch Ugana?" I say to the heat and the stones. "Where is it Mitch Ugana?"

Two men passing by eye me warily. I hear them talking between themselves and for a moment I think they are saying it, too: "Mitch Ugana." I almost ask if one of them by any chance is Mitch Ugana, or happens to know him. Then I see that they were doing their best to look away.

"*Meshugenah*," one of them says. Hebrew by way of Yiddish: *crazy*.

I wonder if I've been had, then I wonder if I really am crazy. Later, when I check out the story further, I will discover that the Web site where the prepuce story originated was a start-up online news company in which freelance journalists are paid by the page view. Its other features are studded with odd—perhaps invented—details likely to drive online traffic. Mitch Ugana? When I think of the name now I imagine a journalistic sweatshop filled with pseudonymous writers—at least one with a sense of humor—churning out news items to ride the coattails of whatever story is currently dominating the media cycle.

Looking over the Mount of Olives, I realize there are no relics here, only a distant small group of men in black. Swaying back and forth like young trees in a strong wind, they are praying over a new grave, paying their respects to an actual body.

Me? I am on holy ground, looking for a souvenir.

4   A Gentle Ribbing

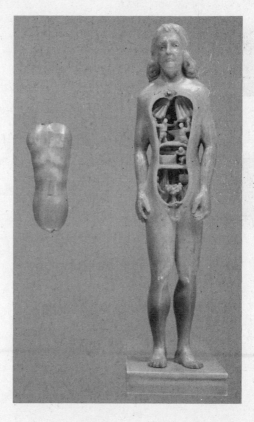

LADIES AND GENTLEMEN, JOAN OF ARC HAS LEFT THE BUILD-
ing. The bits and pieces that may have once belonged to the
Maid of Orleans, the most popular saint the church ever
killed, have been placed inside three glass jars, slid into cloth
cozies, and arranged within a pale wooden case the size of a
toolbox. Setting off on another trip in what has already been
a hectic year, she is taken from the bright lights of a hospital
lab in the French city of Garche out into early evening in the
suburbs north of Paris. While the city did not treat her well
in life, her likeness can now be found on road signs and
church doors and gleaming as a larger-than-life gold-plated
statue in the Place des Pyramids, so she will perhaps feel right
at home. First on the RER commuter train, then the metro,
she rides up out of the darkness like a body exhumed, despite
the unfortunate fact that she never had a grave to begin with.

Joan's companion, Dr. Philippe Charlier, keeps her close
as he weaves through the crowd pushing up from the earth.
A handsome young Frenchman with the slight beard of a
man trying to look older, he has a doctor's respect for the
dead, no matter how long deceased, and so she's tucked under his arm for safekeeping. Up the elevator to his elegant
apartment, she is placed on a table in the shadow of Buddha
statues, Tibetan prayer wheels, and other keepsakes from a
well-traveled life, all illuminated with carefully arranged
track lighting. The contents of the wooden relic case would
make a nice addition to an already impressive collection, but
she is not here to stay.

Dr. Charlier has made a name for himself, at twenty-nine years old, as the preeminent paleopathologist in France, perhaps the world. While pathology is generally interested in the study of disease, the *paleo* part of his chosen profession means that he is concerned primarily with death—the how, when, why of it—and what it can tell us about life, both throughout history and today. The lead organizer of the International Colloquy of Paleopathy and author of *Médecin des Morts* (Doctor of the Dead), he has also opened a lab devoted to the study of historic human remains.

"Once a month we will have an open door," he tells me. "For anthropologists, forensic scientists, anyone who has human remains they want to understand. We will have them put their bones on the table and we will do our best to tell them what we can."

There is not yet a French version of *Antiques Roadshow*, but Dr. Charlier may be the man for the job. So long as the family heirlooms include actual pieces of the family, it would be right up his alley.

"A man brought to me a very old skull with a large hole from gunshot," Dr. Charlier says. "After I told him all that could be known about it, he told me I should keep it. He did not want it near him anymore."

The good doctor places his latest patient on the polished wood of his dining room table. It's just the two of us in the room—three if you count the one partially present between us—but nonetheless it has the feel of a surgical gallery. He lifts the lid on the carrying case and begins to extract its contents with a care that creates a moment of unintentional ceremony. First one jar, then the next, then the next, now catching light from the Buddha display on the wall behind us. Once the glass jars are aligned, we both stand, rising from our chairs as if pulled by strings, for reasons neither he nor I mention. Now we are two men poised around a table that could not seem more like an altar.

Though there is something undoubtedly liturgical about this, I do not feel we are in the presence of the holy. The moment is more powerful than that. Looking down, seeing a curve of gray bone in the largest jar, we are undoubtedly in the presence of the *human.*

"I am sorry for my English," Dr. Charlier says, and then gets down to the business of talking about the rib that may or may not belong to Saint Joan.

✳

THE HISTORY OF relics investigation is nearly as old as relics themselves. In every venerating culture, it has been acknowledged that remains are notoriously easy to fake.

Already by the time of Saint Augustine (born in AD 354, just two hundred years after Polycarp's ashes got the relic ball rolling), there was sufficient call for remnants of the holy dead that less scrupulous clerics sought counterfeits to meet the demand. In his work *On the Labor of Monks,* Augustine complains that his era is afflicted by "hypocrites under the garb of monks, strolling about the provinces . . . hawking the limbs of martyrs, if indeed of martyrs." That there were limbs being hawked was a certainty; whose limbs they were was always the question.

Sometime later, Guibert de Nogent's twelfth-century *Treatise on Relics* told the story of a bishop called Odo who "eagerly desired the body of St. Exuperius, his predecessor." Odo asked the sacristan of the church where the saint was buried to dig up and hand over whatever was left of the body. According to Guibert's account, the sacristan dug up a peasant and sold him to the bishop for one hundred pounds. As the story goes, the sacristan was savvy enough—and the practice of relic fakery was apparently established enough— that he planned ahead by digging up not just any peasant but one who shared a name with the object of Odo's devotion. When the bishop asked the sacristan for his oath that the body for sale was indeed Saint Exuperius, the crafty grave robber replied, "I swear that these are the bones of Exuperius. As to his sanctity I cannot swear, since many who earn the title of saint are far indeed from holiness." Guibert de Nogent writes, "Thus the thief assuaged the Bishop's suspicions and set his mind at rest."

The *Treatise on Relics* goes on to describe ecclesiastics inserting misleading name tags into the nostrils of the anonymous dead; multiple ownership claims to—again—the head of John the Baptist;* and bits of bread said to be the table scraps of Christ. It also describes a "common boy" who died in a village in Brittany on Good Friday. For no reason other than the day of his death—and the possibility of creating relics

---

* This was, of course, not a property dispute; each claimant had a head to call its own. Assuming one of them was the real thing, it's possible that this is the first recorded case of piracy in the modern sense.

of his sad little bones—he was hailed as a saint by a local ab-
bot, who "suffered the fabrication of false miracles" for the
sake of the alms the dead boy brought in for his monastery.

Fake relics were not just a problem for Christendom.
Marco Polo, the famous fourteenth-century Italian traveler,
wrote of Kublai Khan's attempts to procure teeth, hair, and a
"magic bowl" from the king of Sri Lanka. Polo writes that
the artifacts in question were relics of Adam, which had mi-
grated from the land east of Eden to the island off the southern tip of India. However, modern scholars suggest that at
the time, the relics were said to belong to the Buddha, not
Adam. Writing in an era when the Catholic powers of Europe hoped that the Chinese emperor would prove sympathetic to Christianity, and hoping to convey something of
the perceived worth of these objects, Polo apparently jug-
gled the facts a bit to make the relics at stake not worthless
old teeth—as the Buddha's relics would have been seen—but
something his audience could relate to and admire. The king
of Sri Lanka, meanwhile, knew enough not to make the great
Khan angry; he sent the Chinese contingent home with "two
grinder teeth," which were most certainly not Adam's, not
Buddha's, maybe not even human. At the time there was little that could be done to authenticate relics. Things have
changed.

✳

"FIRST OF ALL, the story of all these relics," Dr. Charlier says as
we stand over the bones. "You know that Joan of Arc was
killed by the English in 1431, yes?"

In truth I know this only vaguely at best, and so later on I look it up: Jeanne d'Arc, as the French call her, was just nineteen years old when an ecclesiastical court found her guilty of heresy and condemned her to death. Late in the Hundred Years War, she had been leading French forces in their fight against the English when she was captured outside Paris. Asked to explain her military victories and her practice of wearing men's clothing—considered blasphemously irreligious at the time—she claimed she had been called by God to put on a soldier's armor and drive England out of France, a claim that obviously made the English-financed church court uneasy. Trial documents—including transcripts and a cache of letters she dictated while awaiting judgment and execution—make Joan's one of the best-documented deaths in medieval history.

What the record shows is that the authorities of the church—led by an English-partisan French bishop—knew they were executing a symbol as much as a woman. They feared specifically that if anything at all remained of her, it would be found by her supporters and claimed as a relic of a martyred warrior saint.

And so they took precautions. On May 30, 1431, she was burned at the stake in the Old Market of the city of Rouen, seat of the occupying English government. As the flames smoldered, what was left of Joan was laid out for the public to see, so that there would be no suggestion that she had escaped alive. The executioner then lit another fire and burned her again, and, if tradition is to be believed, a third time for good measure. After this final burning, Joan's remains were

shoveled into sacks. Pious legend has it that her heart—
unburned, indomitable—was found whole among the ashes;
it, too, was tossed into the bag. Brought to a bridge over the
river Seine, the sackfuls of dust, bone, and muscle fragments
were released into the wind, cast into the water below.

Almost immediately a cult arose to venerate her memory,
first among soldiers who had heard of her divinely inspired
bravery, then among the general population. When the war
ended in French victory four years later, her legend grew into
an object of both nationalist pride and religious adoration.
Those who considered her a saint had no physical remains,
but they didn't need them. Thanks to the trial transcripts
and the dictated letters, they had her words. For four hundred years, that's all there was.

"These relics appeared, in fact, to the scientific and historic community only around the mid-nineteenth century,"
Dr. Charlier says. "Around 1865, they were discovered in a
very old house close to the République station in Paris. They
were found in the roof of the house of a chemist—" He
pauses at the word, smiling uncertainly, unsure it was the one
he wanted. "No, no. Not a chemist; *apothocaire*, you know?"

"A pharmacist?"

"Yes, yes. So he had many, many bottles. These bottles,"
he waves a hand over the specimens between us, "they were
with many others like them, some dating back to the seventeenth century."

Dr. Charlier, it should be noted, is not only a medical
doctor but an archaeologist. He does not suggest the age of
objects lightly, because he knows that discovering when

something came to be is the first step to understanding what it was for, who used it, and why we should now care.

"My interest is strongly a forensic one. I try to develop a forensic way of thinking with archaeological remains. Instead of cats or dogs or other animals, I develop forensic analysis methods on older remains because all these cases are very well documented. The death of Joan of Arc is one of probably the most well known of all medieval times. So we know everything about her. This approach will add nothing to what we know of her. Except whether these are her remains or not. This is quite unimportant for history, but for forensic analysis it is very important because it authorizes us to confidently analyze old remains. For me, this case is an *eeks* case. Probably a historical one, but necessary. You see?"

"*Eeks* case?" I ask.

"*Eeks* case," he says.

"X?"

"Yes, *X case*. She is a variable. Whatever the solution is, that is the solution."

"So it doesn't particularly matter to you if it is Joan of Arc or not?"

"Absolutely, no."

Like any good scientist, Dr. Charlier came to Joan both through industrious deployment of the scientific method and by accident. His first use of forensics in historical investigation involved the remains of Agnès Sorel, the mistress of King Charles VII, whose artifacts were kept at a museum in Chinon. A powerful woman of the French court, Sorel had no shortage of enemies, which made her death at twenty-nine, reportedly of dysentery, particularly suspicious. Through examination of preserved locks of her hair, Dr. Charlier determined that she was likely killed by mercury poisoning.

The story of how her remains went public is an interesting relic tale all its own. At the time of the French Revolution, the rampaging sansculottes wrecked churches and every sign of monarchal or religious authority. But, of course, they were still attached to such symbols.

"When the revolutionary people opened the sarcophagus of Agnès Sorel, they forgot she was the mistress of the king," Dr. Charlier says. "They thought she was a saint. This is why they destroyed her tomb. This is also why many people took fragments of her body for medical reasons: her teeth for dentures; her hair for postiches, wigs. And so a great deal of her hair was for a time in circulation."

Some of it ended up at the museum in Chinon. As Dr. Charlier neared the end of his work on Sorel, he visited the museum once again. Looking at a nearby display case, he realized the king's mistress was not the only woman of historical interest behind the glass. There he saw the apothecary jars, set above a small plaque labeling their contents as the possible remains of Joan of Arc. He couldn't wait to get his hands on them.

As a physician, Dr. Charlier treats all the human remains that come into his lab with the care one might give a patient. As an archaeologist, however, he digs through them, sorting the remains and then burrowing into their layers with scalpel, microscope, and an array of ever more complex tools: carbon 14 dating, DNA extraction, even odor analysis. All of which allows him to hypothesize the origins and uses of nearly any object once associated with human life. For him the ways of caring and of knowing seem very similar, and intertwined.

"The original bottle is this one," he says as he holds up a dingy glass cylinder, about three inches wide at the mouth. It looks like an old mayonnaise jar you might find in a suburban garage, filled with rusty nails. "Everything was inside this bottle, which is an eighteenth-century bottle. On the top of it is written: *Restes trouvés sous le bûcher de Jeanne d'Arc, la pucelle d'Orléans.* I translate for you: 'Remains discovered under'—the *under* is very important—'under the funeral pyre of Joan of Arc, maiden of Orleans.'

"So inside, what have we got?" He lifts two small curves of bone, each about three inches long. Holding them lightly, with two careful hands, he shows how they fit together, end to end.

"As you can see, we have broken this bone in two parts to try to extract the DNA. It was already broken but, ah, *sticked*?" He indicates the rough end of the rib pieces, where they apparently had been rudimentarily bonded long before. Running a finger over one edge then the other, he says, "We have to put out the stick to get inside."

I lean across the table and stare down into the hollow core of the bone as if into a gun muzzle. It seems just as lifeless, and somehow as dangerous—as though whatever violence created this artifact is still in the room. Battle, torture, murder, burning . . . what had this bone endured?

Dr. Charlier notices my ponderous expression. He seems to take it more for general anatomical ignorance, which is also true.

"It is a rib, a human rib," the doctor says. "Absolutely a human one, that much we know. And it has been probably, ah, *cooked*. What you can see, you've got the surface of the rib, which as you see is very black."

He turns the rib in the air between us, letting me see all its darkened sides. It is not just black but bumpy as if coated in a mixture of wood chips and sealant.

"It looks this way probably—probably—because when you are on a funeral pyre, your body turns to liquid, then when the temperature goes down, the liquid solidifies, and it deposes on the surface of ribs, on bones, on stones, on anything that is there as a support. So this is what we can observe."

The two probablies are part of Dr. Charlier's method. Even when describing a scene of horrific drama—the saint's skin *melting and coating the stones at her feet*—he tempers it with too-soon-to-tell skepticism.

He reaches into the wooden relic case and produces another jar. This one is clean and sleek looking compared to the apothecary's artifact resting before us. Inside the new jar—more of a beaker with a stopper, really; straight from the lab, nothing mayonnaisey about it—are two other bits of bone.

"I brought this from the laboratory, a modern case," he says, as he lifts the stopper. "So sorry if it doesn't smell good."

Indeed it does not. From this tiny beaker the scent of fried roadkill fills the apartment. The old bone smelled like history—or perhaps that was just my imagination. This one smells of the nightly news.

"As I say, this is a modern case, from a woman that has been killed, and her body has been cooked exactly with the same mode as with Joan of Arc. As you can see on the surface of the ribs you've got the same black deposit, which is muscles, skin, and internal organs. This is quite fresh. Two weeks ago."

He said *killed* but I'm guessing this must be another oddly chosen English word.

"So this woman," I ask, pointing my nose to the beaker, "she was, uh, she *is* someone who gave her body to science?"

Dr. Charlier shakes his head. "No, no, no. This is from a forensic case."

"A murder case?"

"Murder case, exactly. He killed her by bullets and afterward tried to make a false fire."

He who? I wonder, but I do not ask, as we have other matters to discuss. Still I look down again upon the charred "fresh" bone, and the reality of not only her fate but Joan's settles down upon me. Dr. Charlier continues working, however. This is no time to grieve.

He reaches again into the relic box and produces yet another bone, this one closer in color to gray dried wood.

"This is another case, with something quite different, you see?" It is another forensic case, only this one had no flesh when it was put into the fire. The difference between the two bones, he explains, is that one is what is left of a burned corpse, and the other is all that remains of a burned skeleton.

I look down at the two fresh and one not-so-fresh cases before us. It occurs to me that other than nasty deaths, the one thing these fragments have in common is him. One man's interest in telling the stories hidden within bones has brought them together.

"Do you work on all these currently?" I ask. "You are not too occupied with relics for the modern cases?"

"It is often busy, but there is time enough," he says. "I do fresh autopsies in the morning and work on Joan of Arc in the afternoon."

＊

THE PROBLEM OF fake relics goes well beyond bones. Throughout the 1980s and '90s, the Church of Jesus Christ of Latter-Day Saints was shaken by the exposure of forged documents related to its founding. The counterfeiter responsible for the fakes was a disgruntled Mormon missionary turned antiques dealer, Mark William Hoffman, who in 1980 began selling "discovered" artifacts for prices reaching tens of thousands of dollars each. When his works began to fill the church archives as well as the personal collections of high-ranking LDS bishops, he moved on to other forgeries, including letters he attributed to Emily Dickinson and Abraham Lincoln. Fooling his former church was his passion, however. He created and sold ever more titillating documents—including one that purported to show that LDS founder Joseph Smith practiced magic. In Hoffman's most notorious forgery, he presented Smith as a man visited not by an angel but by a giant white salamander. It was these sorts of risks and the theological consternation they stirred up, rather than scientific analysis, that eventually brought Hoffman down. Fearing his own discovery, he killed two of his associates with explosives. He was caught only when a bomb he intended for a third blew up in his own car.

Since Hoffman's time, the business of relic faking has expanded beyond specialized dealers and markets. The ease of buying religious items on eBay and elsewhere on the Web has led to a rebirth in the relic trade and, it seems, to a renaissance of relic forgery. It's not just the distribution and marketing that have improved, it's also easier than ever to pull off a convincing fake. Just twenty years ago it took a talented schemer like Hoffman to create the documentation that collectors since medieval times have relied on to prove a relic's provenance. Today, these certificates of authenticity are easily scanned, manipulated, printed on yellowed paper stock, and sent through the wash to give them just the right wrinkle of age. Many of these forgeries are convincing to all but the most seasoned experts in the field, and even a few of them have been fooled.

Because of these innovations, a number of Catholic ministries have cropped up hoping to police the trade and warn the faithful about fakes. Among the most active is a Texas-based operation called For All the Saints, which publishes the following guidelines on how to buy a relic, even though, as mentioned earlier, relics are forbidden to be bought and sold.

1. Purchase your relic only from a reputable dealer who specializes in relics or church antiquities. (Even here one must be careful, as professionals can be duped.)
2. Never purchase a relic that is not accompanied by an authentication document.

3. Examine the document and compare it with the relic. Is the impression on the wax seal on the back of the relic the same as that which appears on the document?
4. Investigate the name of the person appearing on the document. The Internet has made this quite easy.
5. If you still have doubts, do not purchase. It is better to be safe than sorry.

Not surprisingly, several of these ministries have decided the best way to keep fake relics out of the hands of the gullible is to acquire for themselves as many relics as possible—for testing and debunking if they are fake; for safekeeping if they are the real thing. Based in a small parish in El Paso, For All the Saints currently has a collection of more than forty relics, ranging from tiny bone fragments of the fourth century's Saint Augustine to larger pieces of skin from the twentieth century's Mother Cabrini, which they will gladly lend to your church or prayer group with appropriate ecclesiastical sanction, for a small donation.

Even traditions that historically don't have relics are susceptible to fakes. A few years back, officials at the Israel Museum in Jerusalem were disappointed to discover that an ivory pomegranate believed to have come from Solomon's Temple was a forgery. Unlike the Mormon relics, the pomegranate was not too modern; it was too old.

✳

DR. CHARLIER CONTINUES his guided tour to the possible insides of a saint.

"Everything here is accounted for by a seal of the archbishop in a little bottle, with a paper that says these are probably the remains of Joan of Arc. But the paper is only thirty years old. It dates back from the last opening. You see?" He points a finger to the bottom of the note. "Nineteen seventy-nine."

"So I have to say that we are absolutely not sure that everything belongs to her. Absolutely. This is very important." He moved his hands over a few bits that look like pieces of bone; even after a year of relic hunting, I still rarely know what I am looking at.

"These three fragments are fragments of wood," the doctor explained. "The chemist says that it is not necessarily the wood of the funeral pyre, but perhaps fragments of wood with which the pyre was started. The torch, yes?"

He picks up another jar. Two small bones clink inside like dice. The jar held directly between us, I can see through the glass that the doctor wears an excited half smile, clearly pleased with the puzzle he is about to present.

"This is the most amazing. Here, we've got part of a human vertebra," he points to one bone, then another. "And here we have part of a cat's bone. A cat's femur. Which is very funny for some people because they think that these must not be the remains of Joan of Arc, but for other people they think this is absolutely normal, or logical, because if you go to Rouen, to the place where she was killed, you will see in a little—not a church, but a historical deposit—you will see a black cat inside the wall, quite like this—" He pats his own wall, then realizes what he is implying.

"There is no one inside," he assures me.

I visit Rouen the next day. It is a bit like Walt Disney World, with Joan of Arc in the role of Minnie Mouse. One can stand below a replica of the tower in which Joan was imprisoned, buy three-dimensional molded plastic refrigerator magnets showing flames leaping around a small blond figure, and visit the modern church built thirty years ago on the site of the execution: glass and concrete swooping up like a 1960s vision of the future in the middle of an otherwise medieval town center. I imagine the citizens of Rouen wish it would meet a fate similar to its namesake. Nonetheless, Joan is big business here; the "historical deposit" the doctor mentioned is actually closer to a wax museum, complete with life-size tableaux depicting the life and death of Saint Joan. The hundred or so figures in the dozen rooms look like old department-store mannequins, refitted with armor, sackcloth, or ecclesial robes to play the relevant roles. The official Musée Jeanne d'Arc is a sad and shabby place. There is indeed a cat near the execution tableau; it is a little black puff of a thing with crossed plastic eyes and an overgrown pipe cleaner for a tail.

"It is said the cat was put inside the wall alive," Dr. Charlier tells me. "On the wall you have all the signs that he died inside the wall. Many cat skeletons like this have been found in the walls of castles going back to medieval times. So it would be quite logical to find a cat bone with Joan of Arc. For other reasons, too. To protect from the evil eye, which might come from watching an execution, black cats—particularly male—were often thrown inside the funeral pyre. This might explain the presence of a cat bone—absolutely cat, though we don't know what kind—and as you can see it also has been, ah, burnt.

"Ah, yes, I said *cooked* earlier when I should have said *burnt*. And it has the same sort of black deposit, which tells us it has been burnt freshly. Freshly as opposed to skeletally.

"So as with these fresh cases, we make some analysis on the surface of the rib, then we can know what we can find. The level of sulfur and oil on the rib is very high, for example. We also try to find fragments of insects, fragments of pollens."

I look down at the bone. "Insects?"

He slides a glossy print across to me—black and white with a hint of blue. I see nothing but blurry lines. When he begins to describe what he sees, I feel as though I'm looking at an ultrasound—there is evidence of life hidden here; he traces it with a clinical finger.

"This is a fragment of insect," he says. "Probably a flea. And here is another. When we look with an electronic microscope on the surface of the rib, we can see all these things. With such knowledge, we can approach the place where she was burned, and also the epoch, the year. We will not know exactly. But we will know if she was burned on the northern west side of France, as she would have been if she is Joan of Arc, or if she was burned on the south or east part of France, or somewhere else."

"What tells you that?"

"The pollens," he says and indicates another inscrutable shape on the page before us. "With the amount of pollens and the kind of pollens, we will know something about the place.

We know Joan of Arc was burned at the end of May in Rouen, and so we know exactly during medieval times what kinds of plants, what kinds of trees we should find—if it is her.

"And also with microscopic analysis of tissue, we can approach other vegetation a bit. Not just the trees nearby but the wood that was used to burn her. And also, look here, we can see cells. We can know the coloration of the skin and other information. After microscopic evaluation, we begin with carbon dating. And then genetic analysis. We are waiting for the results."

✳

THE MOST FAMOUS relic exposed to the rigors of scientific questioning is undoubtedly the Shroud of Turin, considered by some to be Christianity's most holy artifact, mocked by others as little more than a medieval towel smeared with ink. Its defenders maintain that it was the burial cloth of Jesus Christ, which miraculously has maintained a full body image of his corpse for nearly two thousand years. Needless to say, many scientifically minded people see in this claim a sacred cow in need of a butcher.

As Steven Stora notes in his book *Treasures from Heaven: Relics from Noah's Ark to the Shroud of Turin*, it was actually a pious purpose that led to the initial scrutiny of the shroud. It was photographed for the first time in order to print prayer cards so that the faithful might pray to the image in the comfort of their own homes. Once the shroud became public, however, it inevitably began to be scrutinized. In the beginning, the scrutiny was not at all threatening to the faith.

Bones were cited as proof that the shroud could not have been a medieval creation, because certain elements of anatomy the image displayed had been understood only in more recent times. The wounds shown on the shroud likewise were said to correspond with recent research that a crucifixion of the kind described in the New Testament would likely have involved nails not through the palms—as Christian art had depicted for centuries—but through the wrists. For a time, it seemed the study of the Shroud of Turin was the best thing possible for its embattled authenticity.

Science—and what it can determine—has a way of changing, however. After that initial wave of investigation into the shroud early in the twentieth century, the scientific community ignored it for decades. It was not until the 1970s and '80s, and the birth of carbon dating and other scientific age-gauging techniques, that researchers began to clamor for the opportunity to go beyond the surface of the shroud and literally into the cracks—between and under the image and the fibers that held it. The Catholic Church finally allowed such a study to occur beginning in 1989. Not long after that, the shroud was found, with very little room for error, to have originated between the tenth and twelfth centuries. It was, as far as all but the most pious were concerned, a fake.

Of course, the problem of scientific "proof" is complicated by the fact that, even in recent times, these artifacts are rarely preserved in museum-quality conditions. Studies of the shroud have found pollens from across Europe and the Middle East, suggesting that it had traveled from one region to the other. However, earlier in its life, it was subject to public viewings, which involved touches and kisses from the hand and lips of believers from as far as the Gospel had reached. Who is to say the pollens hadn't come to the shroud and not the other way around? Even when it was safely in the hands of those who guarded it most jealously, it was far from tamper-proof. All questions and concerns about its authenticity pale before a detail of its upkeep that makes me wonder just how real it is, and what being real means: on at least one occasion, the shroud was vacuumed.

*

MUCH HAS CHANGED in the business of relic forensics since the contentious days of shroud debunking. For the most part, today's forensic scientists don't care who or what a relic *really* is. The point is that it was a person—long gone are the days when a pig's knuckle could be passed off as a saint's toe—and determining all that can be known about that person, whoever it is, is a worthwhile endeavor.

Moreover, scientists are not unaware of the macabre interest their subject holds for many. Charlier's book, for example, concludes with a *Petit Guide Touristique du Paléopathologiste*, which includes around one hundred grave sites of religious and historical interest—Martin Luther, Lewis Carroll, William Shakespeare—in many cases including the cause of death. The full list suggests that he is just as interested in secular saints as religious ones. It seems any well-known life can make a useful "eeks case."

Dr. Charlier is not alone in this work. Other cases presented at the Colloquy of Paleopathology include the fifteenth-century nun Blessed Marguerite de Savoie. Known for her extreme bodily mortifications, she has been studied in death by a group of Italian anthropologists and, peculiarly, animal biologists, who have used her remains as a way of studying the effect of physical stress during life on posthumous tissue decay. The full corpse of the fourteenth-century nun Saint Roseline, meanwhile, has been studied as an extreme case of a body in need of a mortician's care. Restored in 1894 with the use of metal bars and sculptor's clay bonded to her skeleton, she has been studied to learn more about the state of preservation technology at the end of the nineteenth century. Far from being interested only in debunking relics, today's scientists are more often called upon to preserve and protect them. Physicians are regularly brought in to disinfect, repair, or even rebuild tissues damaged by the elements, vandals, or simply the effects of time. Science needs the ancient bodies religion can provide; religion, in turn, needs science to help keep the bodies around a few centuries more. This can range from a mere cleaning and removal of potentially destructive bacteria or molds to procedures that would be considered invasive by any patient, living or dead. For example, the German dentist turned P. T. Barnum of the dead, Gunther von Hagens—the man behind the infamous Body Worlds exhibitions currently touring the world, in which real "live" cadavers are "plastinated" and displayed—claims he was asked by the church to plastinate the heel of Germany's most beloved saint, Hildegard von Bingen. One gets the impression he would love to turn all saints to plastic, all the better to put them on display.

Each scientist has his or her own reasons for dabbling in the remains of saints; as professionally motivated as some of these reasons seem, there is often a personal element as well.

"This to me is not religious," Dr. Charlier says. "The remains themselves belong to religious people, but what they told us is amazing. The archbishop of Tours said to me, 'If it is not Joan of Arc, no problem. You do analysis, then it will go back to the museum.' Because it is really important to know how a false or wrong relic is made. The history of false relics is probably more interesting than the history of true relics.

"I have to tell you I do not personally have any collection of relics. I think the place where a body has to be is in the tomb. Dead people don't need to be a museum.

"I took her once to a church," he continues. "It was to the church of Joan of Arc, here in Paris. I thought if it was her she would be happy, and if not, whoever it was maybe would not mind so much."

This makes me wonder if, in fact, he does care if it is Joan— if he wants it to be Joan as much as the church officials do.

A few months later, when the results of Dr. Charlier's tests come through, I think of him sitting in the church with that plain little box of someone. His tests ultimately suggest that it is not Joan of Arc at all. The remains are much too old. The new possibility: "probably, probably" the bones belonged to an Egyptian mummy. In the nineteenth century, Dr. Charlier explains, there was a fad of mummified materials ending up in various elixirs hocked by, yes, apothecaries.

Ground-up mummies were used as tea, eaten by the spoonful, applied directly to wounds; so widespread was this practice that mummified remains—relics of another place and time—could be purchased by the pound.

An accident of history saw this fad come to an end just as rising nationalist sensibilities in France made Joan a more popular saint than ever. The apothecary had the jar, he had the bones; across the centuries, one can almost hear the gears of his brain turning. Like some medieval bishop stuffing a slip of identification up a corpse's nose, all he needed to do was give the rib a name tag.

Dr. Charlier does not work with relics in order to peel such name tags off. He works with them, it seems, for the same reason he sat with the bones in the church. He cares more about who the relics were than what they are perceived to be. And in this I cannot help but agree with him. Those who believe in relics will rarely be persuaded they are anything other than what their faith says they are; those who suppose all relics are frauds will likewise rarely be persuaded that there is any value in the belief they inspire. Yet for the vast majority of relics, it is impossible, not to mention impractical, to learn much about their authenticity. The best way to view them, then, would seem to be with a skepticism that remains aware of the very real role they have played in both individual lives and our common history. And the best way to treat them is certainly with the care deserved by any body, no matter who it used to be.

Nevertheless, I admit to Dr. Charlier that I find his recent trip to church with the relics a surprising act for a man of science. Taking anonymous bones to a sacred place? Isn't that a little superstitious?

His face lights up at the thought.

"No, no! It was absolutely not superstitious!" he insists. "It was not religious to go there, it was respect."

Just to be clear, he says it again. "I am everything but superstitious! When I am walking down the road and I see a, ah, *scala*— How do you say?"

"A ladder?"

"Yes, yes. *Ladder.*" He smiles, grateful for the word. "When I am walking down the road and I see a ladder, I absolutely go under, each time."

5 HANDS ACROSS THE WATER

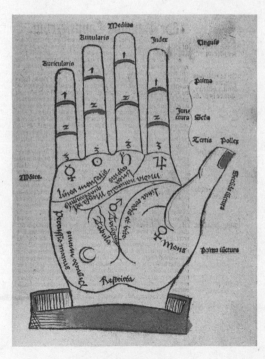

In the small hours of a July night in 1918, Elizabeth Fyodorovna Romanova was thrown into a mine shaft by members of the Cheka, the Bolshevik secret police force that would later become known as the KGB. As both a member of the royal family and a nun of the Orthodox Church, Sister Elizabeth was doubly hated by the anti-imperial and antireligious revolutionaries who had just taken power in Moscow. Beneath her full-length alabaster white habit, she wore about her neck a medallion given to her personally by the czar, an icon with the inscription "Not Made by Human Hands." Along with the clothes on her back, it was all she owned as she dropped forty feet into the pit.

When the executioners heard her struggling after what they had intended to be a fatal fall, they threw another nun in after her. From above they heard Sister Barbara land with a splash—the mine had several feet of rainwater puddled at the bottom—but then the noises of life continued: coughing, crying, praying. Down went the other royal captives of the Cheka: five full-grown men and two boys, dropped one by one down onto the battered bodies of the two nuns below. When they could still hear stirring, the guards threw a grenade down the hole. It exploded, and for a long moment everything was silent. Then, according to later testimony of one of the guards, Vassili Ryabov, "From beneath the ground, we heard singing."

The guards were terrified. The intellectuals of the party had no use for the church, but raw recruits from the countryside that they were, the men responsible for doing away with

Elizabeth Romanova had a deep connection to the faith of Mother Russia in all its gloomy glory. Hearing the consecrated voices drift out of the darkness, they looked at one another and wondered what to do. It took only a moment before they decided to fill the mine shaft with brush and set it on fire.

From inside the mine, "They were singing 'Lord, Save Your People,'" Ryabov said. "Their hymn rose up through the thick smoke for some time yet."

When both the song and the fire were finally extinguished, Ryabov and the other guards hastily filled in the hole and went on their way.

Grand Duchess Elizabeth—Ella, to her friends—was a princess of the German aristocracy who married into the Russian royal line; she was to become most famous, however, as one of a group known as the "New Martyrs": those killed for their Orthodox faith by recent regimes in Russia, China, and Serbia. Numbers of the New Martyrs vary, especially since some in the church venerate as martyrs every last soul murdered from the Bolshevik Revolution through the reign of Stalin, which would put the number somewhere around twenty million.

The Russian Orthodox Church is even more taken with the idea of martyrdom than the Catholics are. Note, for example, the very Russian phenomenon of the "church on blood." When a revered person is murdered for reasons even loosely associated with the faith, up goes a church on the very spot where his or her blood met the ground.

Obviously, very few of those twenty million martyrs have had a church built for them, or are even remembered at all. The church-on-blood practice did not exist during the years of communist rule, when faith was replaced by a state-controlled facade. Though the revolutionary government officially declared freedom of religion in 1918, in the decade that followed so many priests and bishops were murdered that many assumed that any clergy left alive must be employed by the KGB. And indeed quite a few were. At the start of the twentieth century, there were about fifty thousand active churches in Russia; forty years later, there were fewer than one hundred.

Despite this atmosphere, or perhaps because of it, Elizabeth Romanova became a vital figure in the underground Orthodox Church. She became so beloved after her death that she was smuggled out of Russia to a place where her memory, and her bones, might be preserved.

Ella can now be found—most of her, anyway—in the convent of Saint Mary Magdalene, high up on a hill overlooking the walls of Jerusalem's Old City and the Mount of Olives Cemetery, where I searched unsuccessfully for the divine prepuce.

Though the convent is a long way from Mother Russia, it was a sort of homecoming for Ella. She had visited Jerusalem once while alive and was so taken by it that she arranged for the construction of a permanent community of Orthodox nuns. She was not yet a nun herself at that point; she was not even Orthodox, nor Russian. She was the German Lutheran bride of a Russian prince. Soon after her trip to Jerusalem she converted, and not long after her husband's death she took the veil.

It was these stories—the story of her life, but moreover the story of her death, the story of her traveling bones—that led a twentieth-century American seeker to give up her plans for medical school, convert to Orthodoxy herself, and move halfway around the world to become a California-born Russian nun in Israel.

"I went to Berkeley," Mother Catherine tells me as we chat in the courtyard before the convent church. "You can find everything there. Every ism under the sun. I tasted every little pot."

A petite forty-year-old woman who initially seems much larger and older in her black, bulky habit and veil, Mother Catherine talks very quickly, not like the serene nun she appears to be before she opens her mouth, but like the earnest undergraduate still lurking somewhere deep within her habit. Clothing aside, it is not difficult to imagine her among the hippie shops of Telegraph Avenue. Quite pretty in the way that only veiled women can be—her face framed perfectly but for a stray lock of dark hair that often sneaks into view—she has a slow walk that seems an extreme act of the will, as if trying to contain a natural bounce in her step. She has a twin sister, she tells me, who is a television actress in New York. Her twin once had a small part as the pretty wisecracking friend on *The King of Queens*. Imagine the perky neighbor character on a sitcom one day showing up in a full-length Muslim abaya: that's what Mother Catherine looks like. Her smile continues to surprise me every time it shines out from her somber Russian garb.

"I remember going to the different Hindu ceremonies,

and I went to Seder dinners," she says. "It was all very nice, but not for me. The Catholicism of my youth was so devaluated, too. It didn't hold my attention. Then a friend took me to Easter vigil, at midnight, at an Orthodox Church in San Francisco, and I met this nun."

The nun, Mother Catherine explains, had been named for Elizabeth Romanova. One day this Sister Elizabeth shocked the young woman Mother Catherine was then by asking, "What is first knowledge?"

It was a very Zen master thing to say, Mother Catherine thought, but this was Berkeley, where even the Orthodox nuns are Zen masters on the side.

"First knowledge?" she asked.

Sister Elizabeth went on to tell her that everything she had learned in school was only third knowledge. Second knowledge, granted through scripture and the church, was better, but still not the real thing. First knowledge, the nun said, was direct knowledge of God.

"Who had first knowledge?" she asked.

"Saint Elizabeth Romanova," the nun told her, then shared with her young friend the story of the princess thrown down the mine shaft, and the singing that came up from the ground like an unquenchable spring.

At twenty, Mother Catherine decided she desperately needed this kind of first knowledge, the kind that could lead a broken body to find something worth praying for in even the worst circumstances. Broken bodies, it turns out, are something she knows well.

"And now we're here together," Mother Catherine says as

she leads me into the convent church, the place where most of Saint Elizabeth now rests.

"She's as tall as I am," Mother Catherine tells me. "I know because I laid down beside her."

"When was that?" I ask.

"The last time we opened her up."

✳

ELLA'S RELIQUARY HAS been opened many times since her departure from Moscow. Her route from Russia was not the most direct. For reasons of politics and logistics, she came by way of China, where legend has it the monk charged with transporting her regularly had to take her out of her shipping box and rebury her in a hastily dug ditch so she would not be found. More than once, for added protection, he slept atop her shallow, temporary grave. When she finally reached Jerusalem, she was entombed in the crypt of the convent church, where she lay untroubled for more than fifty years.

In 1981, things began to get interesting again for Ella's bones. That was the year she was glorified—recognized as an official saint of the Russian Orthodox Church—a process that, like Catholic canonization, requires an official inspection of the body. Unlike Catholic canonization, which only a pope can set in motion and requires proceedings in ecclesiastical court to complete, glorification is considered to be an act of the divine. For the Orthodox it is the will and devotion of the people that declare a saint, but it is God alone who can make manifest sainthood by producing miracles—such as the secretion of myrrh or other holy oils—through the body.

Glorification is important to the entire church, and so to some in the Orthodox community it did not seem right that a place with so few members of the faith should get to keep such a popular saint. To mollify Orthodox faithful elsewhere in the world, Ella's hand was removed and sent to New York. The nuns of Saint Mary Magdalene convent brought the rest of her up from the crypt and put her in a place of honor beneath icons that were said to weep myrrh from time to time.

It could be said that it was the beginning of her third career. Having been a princess and then a nun, she was now a saint, which has better job security but risks unimaginable in any occupation held by the living. As a Russian saint especially, Elizabeth's body had some work to do, for there was a vast and painful rift between various factions of those who claimed it as holy.

This is where it gets a bit complicated. At the time of Elizabeth's death, the Russian Orthodox Church was as unified and monolithic as the bulbous spire atop Mother Catherine's convent. That changed in the wake of 1917's revolution, and since then the church has become more divided by the year. Until recently, the Russian Orthodox Church Outside of Russia has maintained cautious and contentious relations with the Russian Orthodox Church. Regarding the latter as tainted by decades of communist state control, the Church Outside of Russia has long been suspicious of the church back home. Meanwhile, the Orthodox Church in Russia has likewise considered the so-called émigré church a less orthodox form of orthodoxy. That's the funny thing about orthodoxy: lacking a clear definition by any but its own terms, "orthodox" and "unorthodox" tend to refer mainly to all the ways those who are not wholly in are unquestionably out.

The difference of opinion wasn't only in the minds or pulpits of the church members or priests. It came to a head in Israel not long after Mother Catherine arrived.

"The Moscow church was trying to claim our land in Jericho," she says, "but our superior wouldn't have that."

The superior of the convent knew she had some unexpected weapons at her disposal. She sent her only two American nuns to take up residency in the disputed land and prevent the Moscow wing of the church from gaining control. Two young Americans, she knew, would get much more attention than any number of elderly Russian nuns. Eventually the plan worked, and the convent kept its land—but not before Mother Catherine went to jail, locked up for trespassing by the Palestinian Authority.

"They treated me horribly," Mother Catherine says. "The jailers taunted me about where is my husband to come and save me. They asked if it was true I have never been with a man."

"Did you think at all of Saint Elizabeth?" I ask, remembering the arrest and confinement that preceded Ella's execution.

"Every day," she says.

Mother Catherine does not go into details of what she suffered there, but she does offer that she also thought often of Jesus in his final days.

"If he knew he was doing the right—absolutely right— thing, then he could go through the beating, spitting, the slander," she says. "It was extremely hard but when he was on the cross he knew he was doing the right thing. It's like, you know, I think it's absolutely the best place to be. I think that's what a martyr's death is like."

It did not come to that. She was soon released and the convent won its dispute with the Moscow church. Not long after that, the two Orthodox branches began to reconcile. And when they did, there was one more thing Mother Catherine's convent had that the Russians wanted.

"They approached us about the relics," she says. "An Orthodox religious society first approached our synod of bishops and asked if they could bring Saint Elizabeth to Russia and take her around to the villages. They had done something similar with the skull of John the Baptist.

"So the bishops agreed, in part. They opened the body up and took a piece of the relics for them to take. It's a very big deal when this happens. The bishop was fully vested, they opened the top of Elizabeth's case, and he reached in and removed a small section, from here," she says, moving a hand along her own side.

"He did the same for Sister Barbara. We made a special reliquary for the pieces out of some of the wood from the coffins they were brought in.

"When the Russians came they said, 'Okay, will we need a private plane to bring the relics, or how are we going to do it?'

"And the bishop said, 'Well, you don't need a plane. It's just in this case.'"

The case in question was not much bigger than a shoe box—far less impressive than the two marble sarcophagi where the bodies reside in the church.

"The Russians looked at the case and said, 'No, no. We want the whole body!'

"The bishop said, 'The whole body! Sorry. They're just too precious to us. We don't see this working.'

" 'Okay,' the Russians said. 'How about their heads?' "

The bishop also turned down this request, insisting that only small slivers of the nuns' flesh and clothing would be available. But soon a compromise was reached. They remembered that there was another, larger piece of Ella—her hand—in New York. Bishops in both Moscow and Jerusalem agreed that sending this relic on a six-month tour would satisfy the Russian faithful without further disturbing her remains.

Saint Elizabeth's partial trip back to Russia was a huge success. Thanks in large measure to the devotion the temporary return of her hand inspired, the church of old has come back to life in the formerly communist country. A shrine has been built on the site of the mine shaft; some have said it is as if she has been down there singing all along.

＊

INSIDE THE CHURCH of the Convent of Saint Mary Magdalene, Mother Catherine leads me to the right of the altar. Ceramic tiles echo with our footsteps; it is a vast space usually filled with the convent's nuns and the occasional Russian tourist. At this hour, it is empty but for the two of us and an older nun who keeps peeping around a column as she cleans the floor, sweeping the same square foot the entire time I am there.

"Here she is," Mother Catherine says, as we arrive at a

glass-topped box about as tall as a bar. I look down through the glass and see a tiny shroud-covered body. She may have been the size of Mother Catherine in life, but she is much smaller now.

"She's the reason I came here," the nun says. "When I read her life story, I was so touched. I liked her boldness, her character. She was just so *sure* of her path. She didn't go around things. She went through things. I admired that she could put everything else aside and try and see what truth is. Even in death, even after being thrown down the mine shaft, she found a reason to sing."

All of this, she soon tells me, had much more immediate connection to her life than simple inspiration.

"When I was sixteen," she explains, "I got hit by a car. That's what helped me to make the decision to come here. I had been looking for first knowledge before I knew what to call it, because I had been so close to death."

"It was serious?" I asked.

She nods gravely.

"I flew forty feet up and over," she said. "I was walking across the street and a car came out of nowhere. This woman was intoxi—" She starts to say *intoxicated*, but then finishes more directly: "She was drunk. She ran right through the stoplight and changed my life forever.

"It made me think about what I should do. For a while, I thought it was medical school. I wanted to open a clinic of my own. To own a big building in San Francisco that would have a day care on one floor and medical treatment on another, caring for the whole family.

"But then it happened again. I was driving on the highway, on my way to church, when a car rammed into me and threw me into the highway divider. Other cars just kept ramming into mine; my pelvis was crushed. For the second time in my life, they told me I'd probably never walk again.

"That's how thick I am—it took two of these things to get my attention. Not long after, I came here. Not to join, just to pray. I prayed in the church with Saint Elizabeth's relics: 'Okay, go ahead,' I said. 'I don't know what to do. I'm just here to see what God wants from me.'"

Thrown forty feet, nearly crushed to death, she eventually landed here, and like Saint Elizabeth she has found a way to sing. Her singing comes in the form not only of the prayers offered daily in church but out in the world, as the convent's face in Jerusalem, where she befriends and works with Jews and Arabs alike.

"When I hear the question 'Which side are you on, the Israelis or the Palestinians?'" she says, "I like this answer: I'm on God's side. Of course, when I'm in the Old City they don't know what to make of me, in my habit I suppose I could be a Muslim. So I have a rule: If someone looks at me for more than three seconds, I say hello. And always they are like, 'Oh, she talks!'"

We are now leaning against the coffin, standing and talking for so long it's easy to forget what—who—we are leaning on. She tells me more about her work, her life, her joy at having moved from a famously easygoing place to a city where, she says, "Every day feels like three."

Just then we hear singing. Chanting, really. Somewhat tinny. I look around to see where it's coming from.

"Hold on just a sec," Mother Catherine says. A cell phone appears from within the folds of her habit. My first thought: she has pockets? My second: where can I get that ring tone? My third: it is like a song from a mine shaft, floating out from the dark cloth where she has hidden her broken bones.

She chats quickly and quietly, making plans for community work she is doing in the Old City that day. As soon as she hangs up, she gets down to the business of telling me what she most wants me to know about the place of relics in her life and in her faith.

"When you venerate or kiss or show reverence to an object or the body of a saint," she says, "you give that veneration not to the body itself, but to what the body represents. Just like a photo of your mom or dad or someone you love. You don't talk to that photo, but that photo helps translate your thought to that person. That's what we do with those relics. We don't pray to Saint Elizabeth's bones; we pray to live the kind of life those bones lived, and to die their kind of death."

As our conversation winds down we wander away from the coffin, back out into the courtyard overlooking the Old City. Only then do I notice that Mother Catherine's slow way of walking seems to hide a limp. I ask her if she still feels effects from her various accidents.

"Yes," she says, "but this isn't from that. This is from the cancer."

God, it seems, has recently thrown her down another

hole, crushed her again with the body's endless capacity for fragility. With her recent diagnosis, she will continue to pray from the darkness, but she is also pragmatic about it. Just a month before, she traveled to New York for treatment. She stayed with her twin sister and saw a bit of what life might have been.

"Had Saint Elizabeth's hand been returned to New York by then?" I ask.

"Oh, yes," Mother Catherine says.

"Did you stop in to see it while you were there?"

She smiles. "You know, I didn't even think of it!" And she laughs. "We have most of her here, so I guess I'm spoiled!"

6

THE MOST
DANGEROUS
WHISKER IN
THE WORLD

IT IS THE CUSTOM IN KASHMIR TO SIT A GUEST UPON THE floor, drape him in blankets, and then give him a burning basket of coals to hold between his legs. Kangri, as this basket is called, is not just a basic of Kashmiri etiquette, it is the most common means of personal heating in a place subject to glacial temperatures and power outages that can last for weeks. When not in the nervous hands of visitors, kangri baskets can most often be found beneath the folds of a *pheran*, the traditional ankle-length woolen cloak worn throughout the six-month Himalayan winter by women and men alike. Acting as a sort of walking chimney for the smoldering coals underneath, *pherans* are known for their broad shoulders, sturdy stitching, and burn holes near the waist.

Sitting in the walk-in freezer of an entertaining room of the man whose family has guarded Kashmir's most sacred relic—a hair from the chin of the Prophet Muhammad—for eight generations, I try to keep my kangri steady between crossed legs, but one of my feet has fallen asleep, throwing off my balance. I lean the smallest bit forward to return circulation to my extremities without drawing attention to the hand rubbing my foot, and that only makes it worse. My foot still feels nothing, but the rest of my lower half is not so lucky, as smoking kangri coals spill into my crotch.

All of this is hidden from my hosts beneath the blankets layered over my lap. I'm in Srinagar, a mostly Muslim city in which hospitality is the true religion, a terrible irony given

how much holy killing has gone on here, and so the last thing
I want to do is jump up screaming that the coals have made
the zipper of my jeans as hot as a frying pan.

"More tea?" the guardian of the relic asks. "By your face
it seems you need something, yes?"

His name is Muhammad Busch. Over his *pheran* he wears
two thick blankets, topped off by a knit cap he pulls down to
the wrinkles that give the skin around his eyes a resemblance
to drought-cracked earth. Well past seventy, he is the son,
grandson, and great-grandson of the relic's former guardians,
one of whom looks down at me from a life-size portrait that
is the room's only decoration. The man in the painting wears
a green turban and a purple cloak. He stares with the intensity
of one who knows the future of a sacred object will be the responsibility of the fruit of his loins. Mr. Busch, meanwhile,
has a much sadder gaze, one that knows the line will stop
with him. His son, a tall and thoughtful forty-year-old, sits
by his side, so the problem is not want of an heir. The problem is that the relic now has a new set of guardians: Indian
soldiers. Sent a decade ago to keep the peace, they now seem
here to stay.

"When I was a boy," Mr. Busch says with a grandfather's
smile, "it was my job to walk around the shrine and knock
the snow from the roof. And not only snow . . ."

His son seems to take this line of talk as a polite acknow-
ledgment of the bitter chill of the room. The younger man
rises and slides through the curtain that keeps the sitting area
from the rest of the house, where the women of the family
remain for the duration of my visit. He returns with a glow-

ing kangri basket for his father, who slides it into the folds of his *pheran* without a word.

"Many winters," Mr. Busch continues, "there were long sticks of ice, they hung from the eaves of the roof to the ground, with points on the end, do you know what I mean?"

"Long sticks of ice?" I ask.

"Yes, you have seen such in your travels?"

"You mean icicles?"

"*Ay-sick-els*?" he repeats, a grin coming as he forms the sounds. "There is a word in English for these?"

He looks to his son with raised eyebrows, as if I have just mentioned something newfangled about which the younger man should have informed him.

"Icicles," he says again, enjoying the feel of it on his lips. "A fine word."

He seems to make a mental note of it. His English is impeccable but incomplete, as it is among many educated residents of Srinagar: school-learned, spoken crisply and elegantly, yet pocked with holes. Nearly everyone in Kashmir knows words like "militancy" and "occupation," but some more mundane words have either never appeared or fallen through the cracks. Learning a new one apparently delights him.

"Yes. I would walk around the shrine with a stick like a long cricket bat," he says, "and knock these *icicles* to the ground. I do not know if the shrine any longer has such *icicles*. Perhaps the soldiers break them with their guns."

Mention of the soldiers, the new guardians of the relic, emerges every few minutes in conversation, as if Mr. Busch would rather not mention them but can't help himself.

The soldiers are the reason his family no longer lives at the Hazratbal Shrine, the holiest Muslim site in Kashmir. It is because of the soldiers that he no longer wakes to views of the vast Dal Lake with the Himalayas rising like the arched back of a cat behind it. It is because of the soldiers that the shrine itself—its white dome shining like a second moon at night—has changed its meaning. The shrine, the relic, and the soldiers together are part of what makes Kashmir both "heaven on earth," as it often is called, and "the most dangerous place in the world."*

"When I was young, many things were different," Mr. Busch says. No doubt the winters were just as cold, but his memories seem to be of warmer times.

＊

THE HISTORY OF violence in Kashmir is enduring, complicated, and not easily accounted for by the explanations of intractable interethnic strife common to most places caught in the grip of long-running conflicts. Kashmir is shaped by a unique mixture of religious hostility, rival nationalisms, and lingering fallout from a postcolonial power grab. One of the strangest things about the region is that such a peculiarly modern situation might best be understood by considering a single ancient whisker, kept under glass, stowed in a lockbox,

---

* Bill Clinton bestowed this honor upon Kashmir during a visit late in his second term, which was not long after gunmen dressed as Indian army officers murdered thirty-five Kashmiri villagers for no apparent reason, which was not long after foreign trekkers began turning up without heads after disappearing in the mountains. Salman Rushdie and others later used the same phrase.

hidden behind a gilded door deep within the shrine where Mr. Busch and his family no longer live.

Kashmir is the rugged plug of mountains and valleys that serves as both a buffer that keeps India and Pakistan from destroying each other and a powder keg that at times seems to guarantee that they will. Since the 1947 partition of the subcontinent created two states out of the last bastion of British colonial authority, both Pakistan and India have claimed Kashmir as their own. Pakistan points to the majority Muslim population and suggests that Kashmir is its cultural cousin; India points to the minority Hindu population and says Kashmir should remain part of India to ensure their protection. Most Kashmiris, meanwhile, don't want anything to do with either of these possessive neighbors; they'd much prefer simply to be Kashmiris.

This point was made early and forcefully by Kashmiri leader Sheikh Mohammad Abdullah. In the years following the partition, as it became clear that this paradise was about to find itself permanently between a rock and a hard place, Abdullah called for independence as the only logical solution. And the only logical place for this call to be made, he knew, was the Hazratbal Shrine, home of the relic that for the six million Muslims in the region had defined Kashmir for centuries.

"Certain tendencies have been asserting themselves in India," Abdullah said in 1951, "which may in the future convert it into a religious state wherein the interests of Muslims will be jeopardized. This would happen if a communal organization had a dominant hand in the government and ideas of the equality of all communities were to give way to religious intolerance."

Abdullah was arrested soon after by the Indian government. Though imprisoned, and then exiled upon his release, his influence and his sense of the practical power of religious symbols remained. His political use of the relic ensured that it would be at the heart of a conflict that continues today.

As a relic of Islam in a Hindu nation, the Hazratbal whisker is to Kashmiri Muslims an image of themselves. Removed from its vault each spring on the Prophet Muhammad's birthday, the whisker is held in the air high above the dome of the shrine by a *nishaandeh*, a "giver of the sign." Thousands from all corners of the region crowd the banks of Dal Lake to be near enough to imagine they can see it. That a piece of the Prophet should reside here so far from Mecca, Medina, and the other centers of Islam allows Kashmiri Muslims to feel they are an outpost for the Prophet on a far frontier.

For a time, the whisker and the faithful who revered it existed peacefully among the non-Muslim population. The question of national identity caused some problems in the early years after the partition, but for the most part Muslims and Hindus lived and worked together as well as any two religious communities might.

That changed in December 1963, when on a cold night someone slipped into Hazratbal, broke the locks on the door and the lockbox, and stole the relic from under the guardians' care. The Busch family had been the guardians for as many generations as they had records; no one imagined that any harm would come to the relic while they were keeping watch, but that is just what happened.

Riots erupted in the days that followed. As *Time* magazine reported two weeks following the theft: "After the loss was discovered, wailing pilgrims bearing mourning flags braved bitter cold to march on the mosque. Then grief turned to fury. Next day a screaming mob burned and looted through the capital until police broke up the crowds by firing over and, sometimes, under their heads, killing two and wounding several other pilgrims."

With the wound of the partition still fresh in the minds of both Hindus and Muslims, the missing whisker became a major point of contention. In Pakistan, the press referred to Indian prime minister Jawaharlal Nehru as "the real thief." In India, Hindus attacked Muslims in the streets.

The whisker—or, at least, a hair said to be the whisker—was anonymously returned early in 1964, but by then significant damage had been done.

A generation grew up in the shadow of the theft. Despite rumors—that Pakistan had stolen it, that India had stolen it, that India had stolen it to make it seem like Pakistan had stolen it—no one knew where the whisker had gone. But everyone knew that, ever after, the Indian government, rather than local religious leaders, would regulate its place within local religious life. Kashmiri Muslims resented this control, just as they resented being treated as second-class citizens by a nation that seemed increasingly committed to its Hindu religious identity. Inevitably, they came to resent the Hindus among them as walking symbols of their subjugation.

Another complication was added in the 1980s and '90s when Pakistan—newly emboldened by the Pakistan-trained, U.S.-financed mujahideen's victory over the Russians in Afghanistan—began to send agitators into southern Kashmir. While the Kashmiri Muslim population was unmoved by calls to religious fanaticism, the desire to be free of Indian control combined with this outside influence brought about attacks on Hindus in the area, and then gunfights in the streets with Indian army forces from the south.

The worst of this era's troubles occurred when a group usually described in news reports as "militants" but who the locals still refer to as "boys" barricaded themselves in the Hazratbal Shrine in hopes of retaking control of the relic— and thereby Kashmir itself—from the Indian government. Seventy of them died inside. Not far from Hazratbal, the Martyrs' Graveyard is full of graves younger even than the bodies they hold.

The war is over for now, but the scars of it are everywhere. Bombed-out buildings loom over the shopping district. Indian army officers line the roads at roughly one every five hundred feet. The Indian army makes for the densest concentration of military occupiers in the world, and, according to recent studies, they have contributed to the highest per capita incidence of post-traumatic stress disorder in any region studied. One report suggests it is not just the military so afflicted, but the entire population. Though technically the occupying army shares a national identity with those being occupied, neither side is comforted by this. At the shrine, and throughout the region, tensions run high, which is never good when one side has most of the guns and the other has anger to spare.

"I knew all of them," Mr. Busch's son says with a strained voice when talk turns to the militants killed inside Hazratbal. "They were only teenagers—like me, then. Every one of them, burned alive in the shrine."

Mr. Busch does not allow himself to linger on such unpleasantness. To be so rude as to complain to a guest might acknowledge the reality of life in Kashmir, but it would neglect its heart.

"More tea?" he asks as beneath the blankets I brush burning coals from my legs to the floor. "You are cold like an *icicle*, yes? I can see by your face."

✳

TO UNDERSTAND HOW the hair of the Prophet Muhammad could cause so much trouble in Kashmir, we need to consider the life—and the beard—from which it came. The man himself was no stranger to political turmoil. Neither merely a warrior, as his critics accuse, or simply a sage, as his followers say, he was also a gifted politician, a man with a knack for bringing others together, and a tremendous ego who believed that his own living, breathing, flesh-and-bone body was essential to the body politic.

Before he began hearing voices in the fortieth year of his life, around the year 610, Muhammad was an urban merchant. He was doing quite well for himself in the city of Mecca, traveling often on business through a region governed mainly by clans. Outside the urban enclave his family called home he saw nomadic tribes of sheep and goat herders in a constant struggle for their survival, living in fear of other groups with whom they had every aspect of life in common but no communal ties.

Muhammad had spent his earliest years among such people. His family had entrusted him to a wet nurse who took him to live with her tribe beyond the city walls. There he learned firsthand that the tribes of the area surrounding Mecca regularly raided one another, making off with camels, sheep, slaves—anything that could be carried or made to march away. These raids were so widespread that religious scholar and writer Karen Armstrong, among others, has noted that they were something of a "national sport" in the region. Sport or no, the raids were undertaken primarily for profit, not fun, and prevented a larger sense of community or governance from taking hold in the vast empty lands of Arabia.

It was not the case, as it is sometimes assumed, that the various tribes were separated by issues of divergent religious identity waiting to be united. They all believed pretty much the same thing: the world was moved by local spirits—jinn—who could be either with you or against you on any given day. If the neighboring tribe rode in and stole your camels, the jinn were against you that day. If you rode in and stole the neighboring tribe's camels, the jinn were with you. Far from a belief system that inspired communal living, it basically reflected into the heavens the harsh reality of life on the ground.

The only place one was safe from the whims of the jinn and the plunder of other tribes was within the confines of the city. Tribes gathered in Mecca to trade their wares without fear of attack; as a result, it was also a bastion of civility and peace. No violence or raids were permitted within the close quarters of the urban center.

Inside this safe haven, there was apparently room for a new kind of religious reflection to arise. The city was full of Arabs who had seen the world—or at least more of it than their nomadic neighbors outside the city walls. Merchants such as those in Muhammad's family had traveled enough to be influenced by the "People of the Book"—Jews and Christians—and an indigenous monotheism arose. In Muhammad's mind, the safety of the city and the oneness of the God worshipped there—Allah—were entwined. After an angel came to him and put the words of this God in his mouth, he set about spreading the peace of the city into the surrounding desert.

Once he started making his visionary experiences known, Muhammad gathered others around him, both from his clan and from others. With this new tribe—one defined not by blood but by a shared need for a larger sphere of safety—he began to make camel raids of his own. Only he would give the clans he defeated the option of joining him.

It did not take long before this growing clan began to look for ways to distinguish themselves from those who did not join them. According to the hadith, the collection of stories about the Prophet and his early followers collected during his life and soon after, the one physical characteristic that marked membership in the community—perhaps because it could be cultivated by any man who wished to be counted among them—was a beard.

This was a curious choice, as the divine message received by Muhammad—which became the full 114-chapter text of the Koran—does not require the growth or maintenance of a beard by those who submit to Allah. Rather, the importance of the beard seems to have arisen primarily because the Prophet himself wore one, and he was taken to be the model of the perfect and righteous life in all spheres, from business to battle to grooming.

The supporting reasons offered for beards can be found sprinkled throughout the hadith, which often take the form of quotations of quotations of quotations of those who lived close enough to the Prophet to claim firsthand knowledge of his life, as here, in *Sakih Bukhari*.

"Narrated Nafi': 'Ibn Umar said, The Prophet said, "Do the opposite of what the pagans do. Keep the beards and cut the mustaches short."' "

Here it is obvious that the beard's function is almost exclusively that of group identity. As Islam spread throughout Arabia and the followers of Muhammad encountered more and more people disinclined to join their cause, Muslims used the opposition of the world around them to get a better sense of themselves: Whatever *they* do, *we* should do the opposite. This hadith, it should be noted, is the reason for the distinctive, oddly Amish, mustache-less beards seen on many Pakistani Muslims. They shave above their lips because Nafi said Ibn Umar said the Prophet said to do it.

This is not to say they are moved by frivolous reasons. Quite the opposite: the hadith advocating the growth of beards has been passed through the generations in a chain stretching back to Muhammad. *Chain* is perhaps an imprecise metaphor in this case, as the process is more organic than that. It is not going too far to say that Muhammad is the skin from which the long hair of tradition extended. It grows not so much from him as through him, from a hidden and seemingly inexhaustible source. Seen this way, it is no wonder that the faith could continue to grow long after his death. Even those Muslims who today do not wear beards recognize that the simple act of letting whiskers go untended was once an essential marker of identity and community.

*

NEITHER MUHAMMAD BUSCH nor his son, nor the majority of Kashmiri Muslim men, wears a beard. The day I meet them, each has a bit of stubble, but I assume that is because I have dropped in unannounced and they have a lot on their minds. The only beard of interest to them is the one inside the shrine.

The Hazratbal whisker's place at the center of Kashmir's violent history made its most recent appearance in the news particularly worrisome. In March 2002, the Indian newspaper the *Asian Age* published an interview in which a member of parliament from the Hindu nationalist Bharatiya Janata Party (BJP) questioned whether the holiest Muslim site in Kashmir should be called a Muslim site at all.

According to the *Asian Age* and dozens of press accounts that followed, MP Vinay Katiyar had asserted that Hazratbal occupied a space where a Hindu temple once stood. And the hair enshrined there, the MP said, was not a relic of the founder of Islam but of a Hindu guru by the name of

Nimneth Baba. With this, Katiyar claimed ownership not just of a single whisker but of the right to define the sacred at a time when doing so had significant religious and political implications.

Within a day of his comments, several of the MP's colleagues had denied that the statements had been made, but Katiyar himself issued no retraction. Within a week, the story had spread around the world, bringing international attention to the politician and his cause.

The Hazratbal claim was part of a pattern of similar assertions made by Hindu nationalist leaders. This tendency has found its most volatile expression in the repeated suggestion that certain ancient mosques had a pre-Islamic existence—which is to say a *Hindu* existence—before the Mogul era, roughly the sixteenth through the nineteenth centuries, when much of India was under Islamic rule. This charge has challenged, and at times physically threatened, the place of Muslims within India's diverse religious landscape. In 1992, for example, a Hindu mob attacked and destroyed the Babri Mosque in the northeastern Indian city of Ayodhya. The reason: archaeological reports, trumpeted by Hindu nationalist groups like the BJP and the Vishva Hindu Parishad (VHP), found that the site had been home to a temple of the Hindu deity Rama prior to the mosque's sixteenth-century construction. Similar allegations have created a number of "disputed mosques" throughout India. Since the Babri incident, none of these allegations had received the wide attention Hindu nationalists desired—until Katiyar began making claims about the Prophet's whisker.

The speed with which the international media picked up the Hazratbal story suggests that the addition of a relic to the conflict brought a new, exotic element to the narrative, but the relic had, in fact, played a central role in similar conflicts in the past.

Acts of religious violence on the part of Hindus might be seen as enactments of the VHP's slogan, "Dharma protects those who protect Dharma." To those in the West, this might seem a peculiar use of the word. Outside India, dharma is more often associated with yoga studios than religious principles considered by some to be in need of protection. In Hinduism, however, dharma is the righteous duty one has in life. More than simply rules to live by, it refers to the roles, positions, and responsibilities one has at different stages of life. A Sanskrit term, the word has so many layers of meaning—including a sense that it refers to a metaphysical line drawn around everything that exists—that at times it seems it can mean anything at all.

In the nationalist conception, dharma is intimately tied to national identity and to national borders. Wherever those borders are at risk, dharma is seen as being in particular need of protection. Katiyar's claim of ownership of the hair, while not violent in itself, came from a similar position. According to the rhetoric of Hindu nationalism, it was dharma—that most flexible and slippery of Hindu concepts—that commanded that the sacred whisker be reclaimed, and *Hindutva*—Hinduness—that was at stake.

Yet therein lies a paradox, for unlike most of the world's major religious traditions, Hinduism, as a rule, does not venerate the remains of its holy dead. It views human remains as among the most impure objects imaginable. The hair clippings of the living are regarded as not much better than excrement; the hair of the dead is doubly polluted: first by its expulsion from a living body and then by its proximity to a dead one.

How, then, to explain Katiyar's claim and the seriousness with which it was met by both Muslims who abhorred his statement and Hindus who sought to distance themselves from it?

On the one hand, Katiyar is proof that politicians the world over will say anything to buy themselves a bit of media exposure. The former MP is perhaps no different from U.S. politicians spouting anti-immigrant rhetoric that seems to have been barely considered—or, at most, considered only as a means of sending a message to supporters. Viewed this way, Katiyar's statement is pure politics, an aberration from religious ideals.

But on the other hand, it would seem that relics are symbols so powerful they can transcend the rules of religion. Because relics are inseparable from ideas of the body, and the body plays a role in every faith, even a tradition that officially regrets relics cannot help but be drawn to them from time to time, especially when they so obviously stand for something else.

Both to the Kashmiris and the Indian forces from the south, the Hazratbal relic represents control, specifically control over borders and who has the right to draw them. Despite Hinduism's usual stance on the impurity of human remains, it is fitting that a relic should play a part in this dispute, for the body in Hinduism is considered a border itself. It is the limitation by which we know where the self ends and the world begins; it is the barrier whose fragility grants understanding of the danger of borders and their breach. Proof of this can be found in India's creation myth, the story of Purusha, or cosmic man. As it is told in the Hindu scripture known as the *Rigveda*, this story describes a primeval figure in whom all that exists once resided. Purusha is a giant with a thousand heads, a thousand eyes, and a thousand feet.

On every side pervading earth
he fills a space ten fingers wide . . .
As soon as he was born he spread
eastward and westward o'er the earth.

Purusha is not the prime mover, as Christian notions of creation require, but rather the prime border, a thick line drawn around a map depicting the entirety of existence.

"Purusha alone is the entire world," the *Rigveda* says, yet it is only in the cutting up of the cosmic body that the universe in all its diversity comes into being. In the original telling of the myth, the division of Purusha is presented as an actual dismemberment, a ritual sacrifice in which the cosmic man sacrifices himself, creating the gods first, then all the other bits and pieces of existence. In the bloodiest versions of this creation myth, he is hacked apart with knives.

From this strain of tradition comes the caste system, with its division of life into different classes that draw their characteristics, and their relative worth, directly from the body part of Purusha from which they were born. Similarly, the elements of the physical universe—the moon, the sun—came to be only through the fragmentation of Purusha. The earth, too, and all the regions therein are further by-products of this initial division.

Just as Islam came to define itself in opposition to the other groups in Arabia at the time of its birth—whatever they do, we will do the opposite—Hinduism defined itself as people living by ordered roles in opposition to the disorder of the universe. The point of Hindu religious practice is to find ways of restoring the boundaries that have been transgressed, thereby returning the world to its pure, undivided state. To Hindu nationalists like Katiyar, this primarily means that the nation of India should be officially Hindu from the Indian Ocean to the northern boundaries with Pakistan and China. In Kashmir they see a place where the Hindu borders have been violated. The extremists among them will do anything to regain ground they perceive as lost—including, it seems, claiming another faith's religious object as their own.

*

"HE SAID THIS thing only to cause trouble," the younger Mr. Busch tells me. "The whisker in the shrine has always been the possession of the Muslims of Kashmir. To say it is not is simply to make an insult."

The older Mr. Busch has a nuanced understanding of the problem posed by the relic's provenance. After all, he was there when it was stolen forty-five years ago, and he was there when it was returned.

"Some questioned whether it was the same hair that was brought back after the theft," he says. "Some of the holy men brought to authenticate it did not want to do so, at least not under such circumstances, with government officials involved."

As a consequence of the theft, the Busch family was relieved of the responsibility of guarding the relic. They were replaced by various government offices, and eventually by armed guards from the Indian army. Hindu guards. All of this, officially, was for its own safekeeping.

Muhammad Busch smiles sadly when talk turns to doubts of the relic's authenticity. "Oh, yes, I am certain it is the very same relic," he says in a voice hoarse with doubt. "A very holy relic."

He tells me if I stay in Kashmir until the cold passes he will take me to the shrine personally. He is old now and goes to the shrine much less regularly than he used to. Once, we could have just walked in; he would have used his family's keys to unlock the door, then the inner vault, then the lockbox inside. Now, however, calls would need to be made, permissions granted. The former guardian of the relic is now among those from whom the relic is guarded.

I tell him I will not be there long enough, unfortunately. I must soon be going, not just from his home but also from his country. The kangri coals have grown cool in the time we have been talking, allowing me to brush them back into the basket and rise carefully. I say my good-byes with one foot still asleep.

✳

Hazratbal is a short walk from the Busch family home. When the government took over, the guardians were assured that they would still have a role to play, and so they were relocated roughly the equivalent of two city blocks away.

In the administrative office of the Hazratbal Shrine five men stand over an accounting ledger, arguing about numbers on the page. When they see me, the men confer for a moment in Hindi and then push the youngest among them in my direction. He is perhaps twenty-two years old, with a wisp of a mustache and an awkward air in his drab green uniform. He is not a soldier but apparently the equivalent of a park ranger.

As we leave the office and head for the shrine, he gives a short history lesson. Hazratbal was built more recently than the legends surrounding it suggest. The original shrine was torn down and rebuilt in the 1950s, when Sheikh Abdullah wanted to align Kashmiri identity more closely with the aesthetics of fully Muslim nations. The traditional look of a Kashmiri mosque is actually fairly close to that of a Hindu temple: a tall triangular column rising above a boxy base where the faithful gather to pray. Until the region split in two, buildings and people were Kashmiri first, Hindu or Muslim second.

No longer. Bored-looking soldiers walk the grounds, smoking cigarettes and throwing bread crumbs to the pigeons that fly in dark clouds and fill every square foot of the courtyard before the entrance.

Inside, it feels more like a 1970s American rec room than a religious shrine on the front lines of a possibly world-altering war. The worn green carpet is the Islamic color of martyrdom, but the rest of the decor seems much less carefully designed. Kashmir is a poor region, after all, and the wood paneling, yellow chandeliers, and random strings of Christmas lights seem a struggling people's best attempt to dress up a mostly utilitarian space.

My guide ushers me in, explaining all the while that Hazratbal is a symbol of religious significance to all Indians.

We move toward the door to the relic room, standing inches from the gold embroidered curtain that grants access, but going no farther.

"Is it possible to see it?"

"Oh no," the park ranger says, grinning. "We do not make such decisions here, who sees and who does not."

With that, he is gone. I am left alone in the shrine, except for a woman who lies wailing in a pile at the threshold and a military guard who sits with his back to the wall. Muslim women are not allowed to enter the anteroom to the shrine's inner sanctum, but I am free to wander here and there; he is required to watch us both.

The soldier sits on the floor, looking up at the ceiling, bored out of his mind. There is no reason for him to be here except for him to be here. He is a Hindu from the south and does not have much use for relics.

"It is what they do," he says.

Officially, the Muslims of Kashmir still control the hair beyond the door. The gun in the Hindu soldier's lap says otherwise.

7 TOOTH AND NAIL

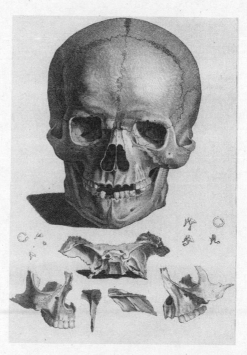

It's generally not a good idea to bring a weapon into a place where relics are kept. In my defense I can only say I never thought of my pocketknife as a weapon before now. The guard at the gate likewise seemed entirely unconcerned, at first. His X-ray machine shows it to be just another rectangular chunk of metal in a tourist's backpack, and he apparently has little interest in holding up the line for yet another whiskey flask or iPod. His supervisor is a stickler, however, so he pulls me out of the queue to have a closer look. Even then—as I pull this tab and that to display three blades, two screwdrivers, and a bottle opener—he seems less worried than impressed. Only when I fully unfold my all-in-one twelve-function utility tool to reveal its other uses does he furrow his substantial brow. All shiny steel and jagged gripping teeth, the pliers seem to settle the matter for him. As I watch it disappear into the thigh pouch of his olive-drab fatigues, I realize my trusty pocketknife resembles nothing so much as a piece of dental equipment on steroids. There is no way he is letting it anywhere near the Temple of the Holy Tooth.

Of all the relic sites I have visited, none have security like the one found in the Sri Lankan hill town of Kandy. Yes, the Hazratbal Shrine had a prominent Indian army presence, but still I came and went from there with barely a glance from the soldiers on duty, no matter that it had been the site of a fairly recent military siege.

At the Temple of the Holy Tooth, however, they have even greater reason to be concerned. Early one January morning ten years ago, as the sun began to rise on the golden canopy that protects the temple's inner court from the elements, two members of a violent separatist group known as the Tamil Tigers crashed a truck through the back gate of the religious enclosure. They drove until the truck's grill ground to a stop halfway up the stone staircase. The truck's back wheels spun for a moment on the moonstone, the carved circle that marks the beginning of the sacred space, and then the whole place burst into flames. The moonstone crumbled to dust, leaving a crater ten feet deep. Eight worshippers were killed, including a two-year-old boy. Twenty-five others were injured. The blast devastated the temple, shut down the city, and drew international attention to the country's bitter civil war. Burn marks can still be seen on the stone walls.

There hasn't been an attack at the temple since, but the political situation in Sri Lanka remains volatile. The week I arrived in Colombo, the capital city three hours on a winding mountain road to the west of Kandy, a commuter bus was blown up at rush hour. The minority Tamil population on the north side of this Georgia-sized island nation feels they should be a state independent of the ruling Sinhalese population of the south. Complicating this ethnic division is, of course, religion. The south of the country is predominantly Buddhist, with a small number of Christians and Muslims living peacefully among the majority. In the north, religious practice is most closely aligned with Hinduism, but they identify primarily as Tamil, one of the many tribal groups crowded together under the umbrella term *Hindu* when the eighteenth-century British wondered what to call the people living under their control. Long story short: the Tamil feel twice wronged, first by Christian colonizers and more recently by the Buddhists, who extremist groups such as the Tamil Tigers regard as a foreign power in need of expulsion.

This is why every one of the thousand or more Buddhist faithful who visit the temple each day must pass through a narrow building that houses a metal detector, an X-ray machine, two folding tables, and a curtain behind which modesty may be preserved in the event of a strip search. As my bag is emptied on one of the tables, I am told the process often runs quite smoothly. When the sun is shining, the locals meet and talk in the queue, all carrying flowers and baked goods to leave as offerings to the earthly remains of the Buddha within. Today, however, a biblical downpour soaks Kandy's streets. Everyone outside the security checkpoint pushes to get into the guardhouse and under cover. Everyone on the inside lingers before moving on to the flooded temple grounds as if they would like to be strip-searched and X-rayed all day.

I stand among them, knifeless but eager to see what many people—mainly Sri Lankans—regard as the most important Buddhist site in the world. Watching giant palm trees dance violently in the wind, I can't help but recall footage of the tsunami that ravaged the island two years before. In centuries past, Sri Lankans looked to the Temple of the Holy Tooth to provide some protection from such catastrophes. Those days are gone, perhaps because the tooth has been proven less than effective too many times.

Nonetheless, the people of Kandy still love their relic. On both sides of me, women point their hands into stupa-shaped prayer triangles and bow in the direction of the temple. With a gray haze of wind and rain concealing the golden canopy and much of the grounds surrounding it, the vista before us manages to look peaceful despite the rainstorm's near hurricane force.

"You go now," the guard says to me, taking my elbow, urging me into the elements. He pats his pocket. "I will hold the item for you. You see temple, then come here and you will have it. Okay?"

Inside the temple grounds I follow the lead of the locals, taking off my shoes and socks to wade through water that has made the guardhouse a life raft in a brown and turbulent sea. It has been raining for only about ten minutes and already the quarter mile walkway leading to the temple is a lake six inches deep. Raindrops splash down into the giant puddle with the force of quarters dropped from an airplane.

Every one of the hundreds of pilgrims and I are drenched by the time we reach the actual temple entrance. Even my shoes, carefully held under my arms in a vain attempt to keep them dry, are filled with water and leaking from the toes. I empty them as best I can as I near the temple stairs, but before I can begin to climb to the entrance I am stopped by another security guard, who points me in the direction of a little wooden building with two curtained doorways. The crowd splits as it approaches the curtains, men to the left, women to the right, and I realize it is a frisk line—female guards for the ladies, male guards for the gents. In the tiny frisking shack we are allowed out of the rain only long enough to be groped from ankles to neck by a burly guard whose dimensions are not much smaller than those of the building.

We are then free to leave our shoes and umbrellas in a far more spacious shed a few meters away. I place my shoes, now as wet as they would have been had I kept them on my feet, on the counter. Five men reach for them with the zeal of baseball fans diving for a foul ball. They all shout some variation of "No charge for service!" with such fervor I can only wonder what's in it for them.

"Your first time to Kandy, sir?" the young man who emerges from the scrum with my shoes asks. He turns, places them on a shelf, and then is at my side before I can answer. I begin to back away, but he is already walking with me, subtly changing my course from the temple stairs to a walled compound across the street.

"If you allow me to walk with you I will be happy to show you everything there is to see," he says. "I ask no charge for this. I only show for the wish of allowing a visitor to appreciate the full beauty and history. After we have seen the temple perhaps you will do me a kindness if you have found your tour enjoyable."

His name is Jacob, he tells me, and he has been leading tours at the Temple of the Holy Tooth for two years. He knows everything there is to know about it, he insists, not only because he grew up nearby, but because he has taken the course the temple offers to prospective guides. He is not older than nineteen but is all business in his white oxford button-down and brown cotton slacks. The pants are rolled to the knees and he strides through calf-deep puddles without an instant's hesitation.

"Come this way, sir. Yes, sir, if you please." He hurries me along, casting glances left and right, as if wondering if there might be a better prospect nearby. I have not yet agreed to be his customer, and so he is risking his daily wage with every minute he spends with me. He is part of an international economy I have seen wherever relics are displayed. Relics bring tourists and tourists bring money and there are always a few locals eager to see a tourist and his money part ways.

By now I consider myself a savvy traveler, however, and I try to persuade Jacob I have no need of a guide. I have come specifically to see the tooth, I tell him, and I'm sure I can find it myself.

"Yes, it is easy to find," he agrees. "But before the temple you should be properly prepared. For your eyes, there is much more to see. And for your spirit, it is better if you are given the opportunity to offer kindnesses to each of the smaller shrines. You may offer kindnesses outside the temple before you offer kindnesses within."

Before I can ask him what he means by *kindnesses*, I find I have followed him through a puddle and to the mouth of a jagged opening in an ancient stone wall. The hole looks fresh, as if a demolition crew has just gone on its lunch break.

"The bomb?" I ask.

"There are parts they are still rebuilding," he says.

"It was a very big blast?"

Jacob stops walking for a moment and stares as if I have asked something so obvious it pains him to know such ignorance exists in the world. He was just a boy then, but he remembers. His family home was fifteen kilometers away, but still the walls shook. He had, of course, been to the Temple of the Holy Tooth many times before that, but it was only then, he tells me, that he began to realize that a place just down the road was important enough to blow up. And if it was important enough to blow up, perhaps it was important enough to help him make a living.

"This way, sir, if you please," he says. "The tooth will only be displayed later, there is nothing yet to see."

✳

TO UNDERSTAND THE Tamil animosity to the Buddhist majority, one must consider that Buddhism is indeed an alien religion in Sri Lanka—albeit one that has been here for nearly two thousand years. The religion itself came from India before the tooth did, but it was the tooth that allowed it to take hold. Since that time it has had a symbolic significance that has kept it at the center of political life in the country even as ruling kingdoms and governments have come and gone.

The story of how the holy tooth came to be in Sri Lanka is older than the country itself. To begin at the beginning, one must start with the tooth's supposed source, the mouth from which, according to a Buddhist saying, "all wisdom is born."

So much emphasis is placed on the Buddha as spiritual figure that it is easy to forget that he was a man with lips and gums, teeth and tongue. In the West especially, there is a common conception that Buddhism is—and the Buddha himself was—wholly concerned with transcending the physical. Some schools of Buddhism even speak of a Celestial Buddha, an image of the universe that depicts the entirety of existence as elements of his metaphysical body. In this understanding of the Buddha, the mind is all, the body just an inconvenient vessel. Yet he lived and died as a man made of the same volatile stuff as the rest of us.

Depending on which view of the story one takes, Siddhārtha Gautama was either a prince so selfless and empathetic he could not abide living a pampered existence while so many others were poor or a prince bored by his privilege, so selfish that he abandoned his wife and week-old son to go on something of a spiritual adventure. Whatever his motivation, the action that followed was the same: the man who would become the Buddha walked away from a life anyone else would call happy in order to witness the suffering of the world and discover what could be done about it.

While it's rarely a good idea to reduce twenty-five centuries of religious thought to a few words, Buddha himself essentially did just that. We suffer, he said, because we cling to impermanent things, which by definition can only be lost. What's more, *all* things are impermanent. We can find our way out of suffering only when we accept this reality.

At first glance, Buddhist relics throw a wrench in the tidy workings of what the Buddha taught. Relics, after all, seem explicitly to deny impermanence. The saint may die, a scrap of holy rag or bone declares, but highly treasured physical evidence of the saint's power lives on. How does this square with the Buddhist assumption that nothing lasts forever? In the first place, to speak in Buddhist terms is to recognize that forever is a time frame too long to be useful for human consideration. Buddha called all ponderings about eternity, life after death, and the origins of existence "questions not tending to edification." In other words, if the concept of forever does nothing for you here and now, why bother thinking about it at all? Seen this way, a relic of the Buddha serves as a sneaky reminder that all things come into being only for limited times. An ancient artifact may seem to have more staying power than most, but in the Buddhist conception of time even a 2,500-year-old tooth exists for only an instant before it turns to dust.

While objects like the Holy Tooth have inspired the same speculation about their miraculous powers as in other traditions, Buddhist relics especially encourage us to ask in what manner that power survives, and moreover what this sort of survival truly means.

It is easiest to grapple with the Buddha's teachings if they are only spiritual. If his lessons contained merely mystical notions to memorize and recite, it would be easy for anyone to live as he advised. But let's not forget how his worldview was formed. At least according to legend, his understanding of suffering arrived while he was on the ground, in the open air. It came to one man sitting on his rump until the roots of the tree of enlightenment bruised his tailbone and the weeds of enlightenment poked through his robe and the cold gust of enlightenment wind blew into his tunic and made him wish he could just go home. The Buddha's lesson is that the distance between experience and the experiencer is an illusion; that he was not separate from the tree above him or the earth below. All of this has a spiritual dimension, of course, but it starts with the body.

As seen in his final sermons, the Buddha knew that his followers, both those then living and those who would later hear his message, would inevitably have vastly different reactions to the fact of his mortality. Some would see in his death a final teaching, an affirmation that even one who so fully understood the workings of the universe was not immune to them. What better way than the death of the teacher of impermanence to drive the lesson of impermanence home? Others, however, would hear of the Buddha's death and would do with his remains precisely what his teaching seems designed to prevent. They would take up his bones and tell fantastical stories about the powers they possessed; they would sift his ashes for anything at all that would assure them he wasn't really gone. In other words, either people would hear his sermons and understand what he had meant or they would hear them and understand the exact opposite.

The Buddha didn't mind this at all; or rather it did not surprise him. He never denied that he told people what they needed to hear to affect necessary change in their lives. He knew that his followers would take from his message the parts they needed most. For some that meant philosophy, for others that meant teeth.

And for those who needed teeth, legends began to be told. The story goes that when the Buddha died in the north Indian village of Kushinigar (around the sixth century BC), his body was cremated according to Indian tradition. Not at all according to Indian tradition was what happened next: as the funeral pyre smoldered, his followers searched the ashes and discovered four of his teeth intact and undamaged, along with his jawbone and a piece of skull. Along with his ashes, these unburned pieces were then divided into eight equal parts to be given to the various kings who came to lay claim to them.

Apparently, the monk called upon to distribute the remains felt he was owed a commission for his efforts. He tucked one of the teeth into his turban and hoped no one would notice. Yet the stories told about the Buddha's teeth were not limited to the world we can see. The legend further explained that the Buddha's death had been noted in a variety of realms, including all those contained in the prevailing Indian mythologies of the day. And so the story came to be told that Sakkra, the king of the gods, snuck into the thieving monk's turban and snatched the tooth away, transporting it to a heavenly realm. Two of the other teeth likewise flew into the sky shortly after they had been acquired, like bits of hail returning to the clouds. One king, jealous of the power the Buddha was said to have, attempted to burn the great teacher's tooth in a coal pit; it shot out of the pit with a force that left a crater. Another tooth had been buried in a muddy ditch; the ditch filled with water and became a pristine lake with a lotus flower growing at its center. When the petals of the lotus opened, out flew the tooth.

After these miraculous ascensions, only one tooth remained on earth, the one given to King Brahmadatta of Dantapuri.

While in his possession, the tooth developed a reputation as a kingmaker; whoever claimed it was believed destined to rule. According to legend, after countless wars had been fought over this small piece of calcium and enamel, a certain prince and princess decided it was time to take the tooth to a land where it might be safe. Early in the fourth century AD, they arrived on the little island of Sri Lanka with the tooth of the Buddha hidden deep within the nest of the princess's raven hair.

Sri Lankan history after that point gets very messy. Successive Buddhist kings claimed the tooth as their own, proving perhaps that the tooth did not ensure power so much as power struggles. By the time the first colonial powers happened upon the island in the sixteenth century, they found a tiny tropical paradise divided between seven warring kingdoms. First for the Portuguese, then for the Dutch, then for the British, it was an easy island to take.

Through centuries of conflict, the tooth remained mostly undisturbed. Kandy is a mountain town, reachable now only by a twisting road that slips through tunnels of recently dynamited rock. Whenever foreign powers attempted to capture it in earlier times, they were inevitably repelled for lack of resources. Though the Portuguese and the Dutch took the coastal regions with a simple show of their naval might, the inland for a time seemed safe.

The British finally cracked Kandy's defenses, and they immediately made a shrewd move. They proclaimed that the tooth would be protected under their rule. As would prove the case in Kashmir two centuries later, by protecting the relic they all but owned it.

A fight for Sri Lankan independence began in earnest in 1818. In the midst of this, the tooth disappeared from the temple. In the decades that followed, the tooth moved in and out of British control. It was finally returned to Sinhalese rulers in 1853 and remained a focal point of Sri Lankan pride for the hundred years that followed. When the island finally won its independence from the British Empire in 1948, the tooth became a symbol of Sri Lanka's refusal to yield to imperial powers.

✳

MY TOUR GUIDE Jacob takes me on a ramble of the outer grounds of the temple that seems precisely calculated to accomplish two things: first, to keep me away from rival tour guides; second, to deliver me to various associates in need of a handout. Along the way we stop at smaller shrines that seem to be overseen entirely by people he knows. "Here it is the custom to do a kindness for the preservation of the temple," he says at our first stop. "This man will take it from you."

He leads me to a small room where a religious functionary of some sort is performing a puja, the ceremony of offering to a depiction of deity. He lights a candle, bows in succession to a half dozen statues of the Buddha, and places bowl after bowl of fruit and flowers before each one in turn. The line between faiths here is fluid. The roadsides leading into the larger towns are lined with shrines and images that are Catholic, Buddhist, Hindu, Muslim, and that combine all of the above. Inside the temple, it is no different. While ostensibly Buddhist, the rituals performed here would be more familiar to Hindu priests from Varanasi than to Tibetan Buddhist monks.

"Here it is the custom to do a kindness for the priest who offers puja," Jacob says. I put a Sri Lankan rupee in his hand and he nods in appreciation to my tour guide first, then to me.

We walk on to a room filled with larger-than-life golden-headed Buddha statues, my head as tall as the largest one's navel, with women bowing before them. A man at the back stands with a broom beside his young son, looking up at me with such wonder you would think I was one of the statues come to life.

"Here it is the custom to do a kindness to this man and his family," Jacob says. "They ensure that this shrine is kept clean for the benefit of visitors. It is not required, but I only wish to tell you the custom."

It does not entirely feel like a shakedown, mainly because I feel that in addition to a fine tour I am being given a tutorial in Sri Lankan economics. Jacob tells me more than once that pilgrims come to the temple because to be near the tooth is to reap karmic benefits. "I, too, receive these benefits," he says. "By working here I am very lucky to receive these benefits every day."

Finally he leads me back through the broken wall, past the security shed, and up the stairs to the temple. As we reach the top I notice that it is not just an informal economy that the tooth supports, but a formal one as well. Donations to the monks are, of course, encouraged; there is a bookstore doing brisk business despite its flexible pricing schemes (a tourist tax, which seems to go directly into the pocket of the salesclerk, is openly acknowledged), and there is a booth offering audio guides of the sort found in every modern museum.

Jacob sees me eyeing the audio guide booth and seems put off, as if I have offended his craft.

"My friend, you do not need the audio guide," he tells me, a bit petulantly. "The audio guide is only for those who do not care to know the real history. And the audio guide will not open certain doors that a certified tour guide might open."

I go to the booth anyway, pick up a headset off the counter, and lay my rupees down. When I return to Jacob he looks hurt.

"If you must have an audio guide then you might do me a kindness now, ah? I have shown you many interesting things and a kindness for my time would be helpful to my family."

He seems prepared to go on, getting agitated. I have thrown off his game, and he loses the assurance in his voice that his tour guide's endless patter provided. But I tell him not to worry. I will listen to the audio guide later, after he has finished his tour.

He nods and, as if flipping a switch, he returns to his script. A moment before his fists were clenched and raised as if he intended to knock the audio guide from my hand. Now they rise up to shoulder height as his palms open to direct my gaze around the room.

"This is the hall for drumming. This inner part of the

temple is the oldest, built in 1592. On the curtain you can see the prince and princess who brought the holy tooth of the Buddha to Sri Lanka in the fourth century.

"The tooth is shown upstairs. Later they will open and you can see the golden casket in which the tooth is kept. The casket will be opening for people only once every five years. In my life I have seen it twice only."

"When will the next time be?" I ask.

He again turns off his tour guide voice for a moment. "The situation in the country is not good," he says. "No one can say when the casket will be open again."

An instant later, Jacob's smoother voice returns. "Do you see the monkeys living high up on the temple wall? You are permitted to photograph, if you like. If you wish to take a better picture of the monkeys we might knock on this door and be permitted to the monk's balcony. It is the custom to do a kindness to the man who opens the door."

✳

THERE ARE SEVERAL other Buddha's teeth in the world today, and all of them are politically active. The political careers of at least two began, as noted earlier, with Kublai Khan's desire to have a relic of the Buddha in China. It is difficult to imagine Genghis Khan's grandson asking for—rather than demanding—anything, but history records that he did indeed send emissaries to Kandy to request one of the prized relics there. He was very likely given a fake—if one doubts the authenticity of the Kandy tooth, a fake of a fake—but that didn't stop it from becoming the most important Buddhist relic in China for about a thousand years, held in a temple near the imperial court in Beijing. In more recent history, the reverence paid to it has all but disappeared, even as its political usefulness has remained.

When Myanmar, then called Burma, asked to arrange a visit for the tooth in the 1950s, the Chinese communists were so dismissive of it that they reportedly replied with a disdainful, "Take it, we have no use for it."

Only later did they realize what a powerful object they had in their possession. They loaned the tooth to the Burmese, then took it back, then loaned it again, then reclaimed it.

To this day, the Burmese so pine for it that they took the step of making a replica—a fake of a fake of a fake, perhaps— so that they could venerate the relic on their own schedule. Though doubtless aware of the questionable provenance of the "Chinese tooth," as the relic is called, the Burmese authorities likewise understand the object's power.

Myanmar has been described as the most devoutly Buddhist nation on earth. Ninety percent of its citizens count themselves as followers of the Buddha, and those who devote their lives to following his path, Buddhist monks and nuns, are held in universally high esteem. The place of the monastic class in society is reinforced once a year when the replica tooth relic is removed from its shrine in the town of Paungde. Placed on the back of an elephant, the relic is then paraded through the city to bestow blessings on all who behold it. Thousands of monks and other devotees follow in procession, filling the streets with burgundy robes, the smell of incense, and the cacophony of drums, gongs, and chanted prayers.

The scene seems as though it could have occurred a thousand years ago, but it has been going on for only half a century. In a country with an uneasy relationship between religious authorities and the governing military junta, the parade has become a display of the ambivalent nature of relics as tools of both piety and power. While the Paungde procession looks like an entirely religious affair, in fact the state controls the relic. By carefully orchestrating its use, the state also hopes to control the influential monastic population, which cannot help but venerate the tooth, no matter who holds the keys to its temple.

As in Sri Lanka, however, it seems the meaning of the tooth as a political symbol is changing in Myanmar. Around the same time I was in Kandy touring the Temple of the Holy Tooth, the monks of Myanmar decided to call off their yearly procession in Paungde. Flexing their organizational muscles in a new way, the monks moved their gathering one hundred miles to the south to the city of Yangon, where for the first time they engaged in large-scale protests against the government. As newspapers around the world reported, they withstood a violent response from the military even as they rallied the people to their defense.

✳

AFTER A SOLID hour of talking and pointing, Jacob delivers me to the stairs that lead to the puja hall, where the nightly display of the relic casket is held. He indicates that his tour is completed and it is time at last to show him a kindness. I thank him as I fold a pile of rupees into his hand. He nods with his fee held before him in a prayerful gesture that he seems to use as both a sign of sincere gratitude and a subtle way of making sure the stack of bills is sufficiently thick. He must think it is, because he keeps talking for a few minutes more, off the clock.

"What you must understand about the tooth is that it is the symbol of Sri Lanka," he says. "In childhood we are taught the history of the tooth and what it has done for our people. And we are taught that it was attacked. We learn that those who attack the tooth attack us. When it is prayed to, this is what is prayed to. When it is protected, this is what we protect."

With that, Jacob says the quickest of good-byes and hurries across the room to another befuddled-looking tourist. In another place, I realize he would make a great politician. He has histories to relate, a local economy to stimulate, and a cause to stump for, all of it captured perfectly by a single, ancient tooth.

✳

THE PUJA HALL is entirely made of wood except for the silver-plated door that is its focal point. The wood is painted red, yellow, green, and orange—the colors of the Sri Lankan flag—and the hundreds who crowd in to pay respect to the relic are nearly all local. They have been here before—which I've found is rare at relic sites around the world—and they will all be back within a week or two. Attendance at the Temple of the Holy Tooth dropped briefly in the immediate aftermath of the Tamil attack, but it quickly rebounded and then became larger than ever. The increased security has made the locals' visits even more meaningful; now they can be proud not only that the Buddha's tooth is in Kandy, but that they have kept it safe during what is arguably the most dangerous time in its history.

The crowd pushes in around me and I am moved as if by a wave, first toward the relic chamber, then away, then toward it again. From somewhere nearby in the temple, the ceremonial music has begun: three competing drums and a sirenlike flute that would sound like snake-charming music if the point of snake charming was not to calm the snakes but to whip them into a frenzy. With three different rhythms and no apparent melody, at least to my Western ears, it is a maddening and endless sound track to the mob scene in which I have suddenly found myself.

After a few more minutes of moving with the tide of the faithful, I spot up in the corner of the puja hall a roped-off queue that seems to lead to the relic chamber. Moving through this crowd, I realize, is a bit like shooting the rapids; one can only throw one's raft into the current and hope for the best. I see a family led by a stout and determined father, and I allow myself to be drawn along in their wake.

I follow them all the way to the relic chamber. Inside, there is a small room filled with monks. They are not meditating or praying; they seem just to be hanging out, sitting in flowing, electric orange robes with knees and nipples exposed. Ostensibly they are there to guard the tooth. They look like they're sitting in a sauna. And, sure enough, the room does seem filled with a holy glow, emanating from the golden tooth casket at the back of the room. Cylindrical but with a pointed top like a model spaceship, the casket stands as tall as I am, about twenty feet away from the closest point the faithful and the curious are allowed to stand. After just five seconds a burly monk lifts his hand and holds it before my face, letting me know it's time to move on.

✳

THE RAIN HAS stopped and the sun is setting as I leave the temple. The walkway to the exit is puddled with shin-high water. I decide to head for the nearest exit and have one foot through a gate marked "No Reentry" when I remember my pocketknife. I am leaving Kandy that night, and so I know I will not be able to return for it the next day.

Back at the main entrance, pilgrims continue to stream in barefooted, holding umbrellas as they pass through the metal detectors. None of the guards I saw earlier remains on duty, so when I ask about my pocketknife I am met by blank stares. Finally, I catch the supervisor's eye. He seems to remember me and calls out something in Sinhalese, at which one guard nods, leaves his post, and sets off through the puddles, toward the temple. Another guard says to me, "This way."

He leads me to a small security shed empty but for a few battered seats and a bank of video screens displaying the contents of bags X-rayed outside. The guard moves a rifle off a pink plastic beach chair and says, "Sit."

After five minutes, I ask if the other guard has gone to another office; is there a place where they keep confiscated materials?

"No worry, sir," the guard says.

After ten minutes I wonder if perhaps he needs a description of what I am looking for. I dig through my guidebook for a dictionary and try out the word I find, "*Pihiay?*" I say. "*Pihiay?*"

Another guard joins us as I say it four or five more times with variations in emphasis and intonation. They stare at me with widening eyes until I realize that in the unlikely event that I am saying the word correctly, I am sitting with two armed guards ten thousand miles from home shouting "Knife! Knife! Knife! Knife!" If I am saying it incorrectly, on the other hand, I am sitting with two armed guards ten thousand miles from home shouting a word that means who knows what, or nothing at all.

"No worry, sir," the second guard says.

After half an hour it becomes clear that the guards I am sitting with have no idea why I am there. They have begun to be amused by my presence, however, and begin to talk between themselves in Sinhalese, apparently conferring to decide what they should ask this foreigner who has come to visit the home of the symbol of their nation. My Sri Lankan interrogation goes something like this:

"You like Sri Lanka food?"

"Yes, yes . . . very spicy."

"You like Sri Lanka weather?"

"Yes, yes. . . . Maybe a bit too rainy."

"You like Sri Lanka relic?"

"Yes, yes . . . very powerful relic."

They look at each other and trade a few words I imagine to be something close to "You ask him," "No, you ask him."

Finally, the first guard gathers his courage and he says to me: "You like Sri Lanka . . . girls?"

They bubble up with laughter, falling into each other, letting their rifles fall against the wall.

They are, I realize, all of nineteen or twenty years old. Behind them, the images on the X-ray screens roll by one after another. Who knows what dangers are slipping into the Temple of the Holy Tooth amid all this cross-cultural hilarity?

They're still tittering when a third guard appears at the door with my all-in-one utility knife in his outstretched hand. I say good-bye to the laughing temple guards, accepting a Buddhist blessing from them, and offering the same.

They will need it more than I will, I think. They are all that is standing between the Buddha's tooth and disaster.

8 SPLITTING HAIRS

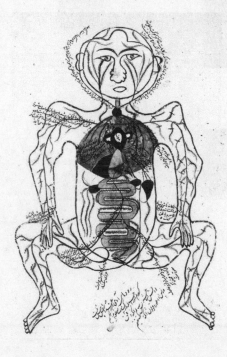

From a few yards away, a bucket of severed sheep heads is nearly indistinguishable from a bucket of pickles: same white plastic tub, same gray metal handle, same slosh of brine spilling over the side. It's only on closer inspection, when you peer into the murky juices, that the differences become apparent. To begin with, the contents of a pickle bucket do not stare back. Mouths open, nostrils flared, severed sheep heads look up at you as if ready to sing.

I make this discovery deep within the sprawling marketplace of the Aleppo souk, the smelly heart of a Syrian city that claims to be the oldest continually inhabited urban area in the world. After spending a few hours wandering its twenty miles of covered streets, I know I could find almost anything among its thousands of merchant stalls. The souk was the center of the city even in Roman times, and it seems lots of what is on offer hasn't changed much since then. By the end of the day, I am weighed down with woven tablecloths, bags of homemade algae-green olive oil soap, a menagerie of questionably antique elephant and turtle figurines, and enough *shawarma* to make me wonder what animal or combination of animals could be so easily transformed into a rotating column of meat. The air hangs thick with the sweet burned-apple smell of water-pipe smoke and the sharper scents of sweat, spices, and steaming samovars. Lost in this maze of a premodern shopping mall, I find the sheep heads a little unsettling, but they seem right at home.

A man in a bloody apron catches me squinting at his wares.

"*Deutsch?*" he calls. "*Français? Anglais?*"

"American."

"Hello, America!" he cheers, flashing a grin that shows no hint of hard feelings despite the often uneasy relationship between our countries. Then he waves his hand in the direction of his buckets, fluttering his fingers in a circular motion over the available condiments as if to indicate that I don't need to choose between pickles, onions, cabbage, and sheep heads. Yes, his smile says. I could have them all.

"You eat something, Mister America?"

Tempting as it is, I thank him and walk on, in search of a head of another kind.

Nearly every Syrian guidebook explains that the uppermost remains of Zacharias, father of John the Baptist, can be found in Aleppo's Great Mosque, which has one of its entrances immediately off the souk.

Like the sheep heads on sale at the Aleppine equivalent of a fast food stand, the fact that an obscure character from Christian history should be the object of Islamic veneration is at first surprising, but then makes its own kind of sense. As a faith that regards itself as the last in the succession of monotheist religions, Islam has a long tradition of incorporating the major and minor figures of Judaism and Christianity into its own devotional practices. Islam calls them all prophets, adopting them into a genealogy of gradually unfolding prophecy that, Muslims believe, began with Adam and ended with Muhammad. Down through the centuries, Islam has not only absorbed the memories and the stories of these retroactive prophets, it has also borrowed their bones.

Aleppo's main mosque, also known as *al-Jami al-Kabir*, is one of a number of sites in Syria that claim to be the final resting place of men and women mentioned in the Bible. The Great Mosque of Damascus, *al-Jami al-Ulawi*, likewise is well known as home to a prominent New Testament head, namely the always popular one that Salome ordered removed from John the Baptist's body.* A short drive to the west, near Syria's border with Lebanon, one can find the enshrined resting place of Adam's son Abel, who, at least according to accounts in Genesis and the Koran, was the first human to die, and thus also the first to be buried.

There are tombs of other well-known biblical figures throughout the Muslim world: Job, Cain, Ishmael, Seth, Joshua, Aaron, Hosea . . . the full list would fill several pages of *begats*. Prophets who in Judaism and Christianity are remembered with words alone have in Islam been given bodies and grave markers.

Several of the most important of these ancient Hebrews are believed to be buried with other prophets of Islam in Mecca, a few in the Kaaba itself, the huge black monolith around which Muslims walk at the end of their pilgrimage to their holy city. These tombs of Hebrew prophets are at the symbolic center of Islamic faith.

The final resting places of Adam and Eve, meanwhile,

---

* As it happens, Damascus and Aleppo have long been engaged in a disagreement as to which of these two ancient cities can call itself the longest continuously inhabited city in history. With this in mind, it's possible that Aleppo's claim to have the head not of the Baptist but of his father is a sort of interurban holy-dead one-upmanship.

remain in dispute. One strain of Islamic tradition holds that, in addition to two elephants, two turkeys, two hyenas, and all the rest, Noah loaded onto his ark the disinterred remains of the parents of humanity, as if they, too, would have procreation to attend to after the flood. Once the waters had receded, this legend holds, Noah reburied both Adam and Eve in Jerusalem. Another tradition begs to differ: depending on who you ask, Eve may be buried in Jidda, Saudi Arabia, or due north in the Baaqa Valley. Adam's head may be at the Mosque of Abraham in Hebron, Jordan, while his legs may be buried under the Dome of the Rock in Jerusalem.

Islam makes no comment on the Christian claim that Adam's skull is, in fact, buried under the site of Jesus's crucifixion, but there certainly would have been enough of him to go around. A unique element of Islamic remembrance of the holy dead is that its prophets are often described as having been truly larger than life. After his exile from the Garden of Eden, for example, Adam is said to have been sixty cubits tall—just shy of one hundred feet. Before the fall, the story goes, he was even taller than that.*

---

* It seems that each generation after the fall became shorter. By the time Joshua arrived on the scene, for example, he measured only five meters. According to certain strains of Islamic tradition, this downsizing occurred not only in humans but in every element of the physical world with which humans had contact. The *Alice in Wonderland* images summoned by this can be found in Muslim commentaries on the Bible, in which it is explained that a single granule of grain was larger than an ostrich egg in Adam's time, but only the size of a chicken egg in the time of Elijah, forty generations later.

Such gigantic bodies naturally led to gigantic tombs. Scattered throughout the Islamic world, not just in the Middle East but also in Southeast Asia, ancient grave sites of dozens of biblical figures, and others important to the early Muslim faithful, have (or once had) the appearance of coffins as long as tractor trailers. In some cases, according to legend, they began the size of SUVs and grew miraculously through the years. It is reported that Job's coffin, before it was lost to history, was twelve feet long. The tomb of Seth, Adam and Eve's third son, was seventeen feet long. The grave of Eve in Jidda once was said to measure almost two hundred yards, a fact that caused no end of wonder to the nineteenth-century British traveler and poet Charles Montagu Doughty. Upon seeing Eve's colossal resting place, Doughty supposed that the "great mother's navel" must have been "more than the height of a great cedar," her children "greater than elephants" at birth. "If this were the first woman," he asked with admiration and awe, "what should Adam be?"

The reasons given for these giant graves are as numerous as the dead they commemorate. Some traditions hold that the graves were enlarged by the power of the bodies they contained, as if the lives they had lived were undiminished by death. Others claim that the endless stream of pilgrims visiting the tombs somehow expanded the bodies of the dead through their devotions. More practical explanations have included the simple admission that, at the time of the grave's consecration, no one remembered exactly where the bones of the holy one lay.

The holy dead have obviously inspired much thought among some Muslims. For others, however, offering any reverence to the physical remains of even the most revered (or the largest) ancestors is forbidden, creating a devotional impasse that has presented no small problem in much of the Islamic world. Among the most telling examples: the tomb of Eve that provoked such a perplexed reaction from Mr. Doughty in the 1870s was covered with a concrete slab by Saudi religious authorities in 1975. It remains covered today.

That such a seemingly impious act could be performed for pious reasons highlights the most pressing challenge facing Islam today. Because they are not universally embraced, relics are at the center of the doctrinal divide that separates one kind of Muslim from another. No matter their size or holiness, the bodies of the dead are considered unclean in Sunni Islam, and any association with them is to be avoided—aggressively so in Sunni-dominated states like Saudi Arabia, where no less than three hundred relic-related sites have been demolished in the past fifty years. On the other hand, among Shia Muslims, a quarter of the Syrian population, relic veneration remains a vital element of the faith.

This breach within the religion is most likely a lingering echo of the ancient dispute that turned Islam into the house divided it remains today. In the years following the Prophet's death in 632, some believed that his nephew Ali, who had been among the first to believe Muhammad's prophetic claims, was his proper successor. Others believed the Prophet should have no successor; when he was gone he was gone. There remained nothing of him in this world, not his body and not his authority, and it was dangerous to propose otherwise.

Not surprisingly, it was those who embraced Ali—the Shiites—who came to venerate relics, just as those who opposed him—the Sunnis—now regard relics as damaging to the faith. In this sense, the mythic proportions of certain prophets says as much about their size and importance to the Muslim imagination as it does about the legends of their supernatural abilities and accomplishments. The question of the height of a long-dead holy man may seem a bit silly, but the differences of belief it implies, as we in our own era are reminded, remain the stuff of which wars can be made.

✳

I HAVE NO idea how tall Zacharias was supposed to be. If he was anything like the other plus-sized prophets of Islam, I guess that if I walk the souk long enough, I will find him.

But where to look among all this merchandise? Past the spice dealers, the jewelry hockers, and the carpet salesmen, I wander searching for either a way into the mosque or just a path out of the souk. Finally I spot a group of four women, covered head to toe in flowing black abayas, moving deliberately through the crowd, though not in such a rush that they don't pause here and there to browse the textiles and the children's clothing. I follow them like a fisherman who spots a dark mass moving beneath the waves. When they turn suddenly and push through an unexpected set of carved wooden doors, I do the same.

From the crowd and bustle of the souk, I enter a cooling calm that offers immediate relief. An expanse of green carpet stretches down a few stairs and then to the left and the right, filling a room as large as a football field. Though technically the souk is outdoors and the mosque is in, the former hung with the stale air of commerce, while the latter has an atmosphere that feels as exposed and open as a mountaintop. I stand in the doorway while a breeze blows from inside to out, a puff of musky mosque wind that sways the shirts and dresses in the tailors' stalls behind me.

The veiled women slip off their shoes and descend the steps. I follow, so surprised to find myself now in echoing silence after the noise of the souk that I nearly tumble down the stairs. I look to my left and see a crowd gathered, men divided from women, all milling about, reaching their hands toward the wall.

I have moved only a few steps toward them when I hear a sound like a tire losing air above me: *sssst, sssst, sssst.* And then I see its source: a bearded man in an ankle-length beige robe, descending the steps of the minbar, a pulpit sitting atop a steep stairway. From his robe and officious air, I guess he is the muezzin, the man charged with making the call to prayer five times each day, who is also responsible for the general upkeep of the mosque. He wags a finger at me, points at my feet, then points to the door. Flustered, I spin on my heels and retreat ten quick steps to the souk and the maze from which I was grateful to emerge.

I am back to the sheep heads before I realize the muezzin was only pointing at my shoes, which I neglected to remove as I took my first step down the stairs.

"Mister America!" the butcher calls. "You come back to eat? Or for what do you look?"

I turn to retrace my steps but by then it is too late. Looking ahead to a dozen possible routes through the avenues of merchant stalls, I can't remember which turns had taken me to the mosque entrance.

"Tell me, my friend! What do you look?"

"Zacharias's head?" I answer.

The butcher squints at me as if unsure of his English, crinkling his brow with a look that seems to say, *Sheep heads? Yes. Prophets' heads? No.* Nonetheless, he aims to please; if he couldn't help me find my way, he would at least make sure I was well fed.

"*Shawarma?*" he says.

✳

WHILE CHRISTIANITY POSSESSES a larger relic inventory than any other faith, Islam has the distinction of revering relics earliest within its own history. According to some strains of Islamic tradition, as explained by religious historian Brannon Wheeler, whose book *Mecca and Eden* served as a guidebook of sorts to the relics of Syria, the Prophet Muhammad's followers began venerating pieces of him even while he was alive.

It's said that after his pilgrimage to Mecca, Muhammad cut his hair and trimmed his fingernails, then instructed Abu Talhah, first among the original devotees often called the companions, to distribute a few clippings to each of the men who had accompanied him on his journey to the holy city, the original hajj. He then asked Abu Talhah's wife to give the rest to the women to divide among themselves.

Other reports suggest that the distribution was not so orderly, as in the nineteenth-century biography of Muhammad by Seyyid Ahmed Zaini Dahlan: "When the Prophet had his head shaved and his companions surrounded him, they never suffered a single hair to fall to the ground but seized them as good omens or for blessing. And since his Excellency only had his hair cut at times of the pilgrimage this had become *sunna* [law] and he who denies it should be severely punished."

And it didn't stop with his hair. One of Muhammad's earliest followers, Anas, is said to have reported this account of how he came into possession of a jar full of the Prophet's sweat. He got it, he said, from his mother, Umm Sulaym. "The Prophet stayed with us, and as he slept my mother began to collect his perspiration in a flask. The Prophet awoke and said: 'O Umm Sulaym, what are you doing?' She said: 'This is your sweat which we place in our perfume and it is the best perfume.'"

Some hadith report that even Muhammad's washing water was prized. The companions vied for the honor of collecting the contents of his ablution basin so that they could put it on their faces. The names of more than one hundred early followers who received this and similar blessings of spit are recorded and remembered with great honor.

At least according to some accounts, Muhammad invited this sort of physical reverence. He regularly healed the sick with his saliva and commanded that all the new mothers in Medina bring their infants to him so that he could bless them a blow of *nafth* and *tifl*, breath mixed with saliva. Only the most forward thinking of these mothers, apparently, figured out a way to save some of the Prophet's spit for later.

Regardless of how they were acquired, evidence of these bodily keepsakes can be found in accounts of the deaths of early Muslim leaders. As he lay dying, the first caliph of the Umayyad dynasty, Muawiyah, told his son: "The apostle of God once clothed me with a shirt, and I put it away. He pared his nails one day, and I took the parings and put them in a bottle. When I die, clothe me in that shirt, cut up and grind the parings, and scatter them on my eyes and mouth so that God might perhaps be merciful to me on account of the blessings of these things."

While he lived, Muhammad was a well-traveled man, but his clippings logged even more miles. Other accounts place his hair and/or fingernails in the Syrian city of Homs, in Kairouan in Tunisia, and at various places throughout Egypt. A certain Jafar ibn Khinzabu, vizier of an Egyptian prince, left instructions that his three hairs of the Prophet be placed in his mouth upon his death and carried within him to the city of Medina, site of Muhammad's tomb.

In time it seems the hairs became too valuable to be buried. As the early Muslim commentator Mohammed bin Darian wrote: "I said to Obeid al Suleimani, 'I have a few hairs of the Prophet which I took from Anas,' and he replied, 'If I had but a single hair it would be more to me than the whole world.'"

As prized possessions and status symbols at a time when both the wealth and influence of Islamic civilization were on the rise, relics were often displayed as evidence of one's power. And because they were worth so much, it was perhaps inevitable that they would begin to multiply. A traveler by the name of Abdul Jani ul-Nabulusi tells of meeting a Muslim from India, Ghulam Mohammed.

> He told me that in the countries of India many people possess the Prophet's hair, many have but a single hair, but others own more, up to twenty. These relics are shown to all those who would inspect them reverently. This Ghulam Mohammed tells me that one of the saintly men of the lands of India annually exhibits such relics on the ninth day of Rabi-ul-Aval, that on those occasions many people gather around him, learned and pious, perform prayers to the Prophet and go through divine service and mystic practices. He further informs me that the hairs sometimes move of their own accord, and that they grow in length and increase in number, so that a single hair is a propagator of new ones.

Through the years, it became less and less likely that every one of the hundreds of relics of the Prophet that once existed were authentic, but authenticity also became less important. As the fame of the relics spread, mosques, shrines, and communities of devotion sprang up around them, and these soon became the destination for pilgrims who could not make the more auspicious and difficult pilgrimage to Mecca. As such, each site became a kind of mini-Mecca in its own right.

Perhaps Muhammad knew this would happen when he allowed his hairs and nail clippings and ablution water to be gathered. With parts of him spreading out wherever his followers traveled, it no longer mattered whether Muhammad went to the mountain or the mountain came to him. Through his relics, there was nowhere he couldn't be and nowhere his followers couldn't find him.

✳

BACK OUT IN the streets of Aleppo, I remember that it is June. The heat hanging over the city makes even the dirty water in the gutters seem to sizzle, giving empty streets a constant white-noise hum. And the temperature feels intensified by the coverings of the women who walk by—not just hijabs and abayas but full, ankle-length burkas leaving no trace of skin exposed. Even their fingers are wrapped—a fact I didn't realize until a woman with a covered face held out a begging hand in a black nylon glove. I sweat through my shirt the moment I step out of the cool of the mosque. Even leaving all questions of the propriety or fairness of such restrictive religious coverings aside, I don't know how these women manage to survive.

Of course, survival is relative—in life, religion, and politics as well. A few weeks before my arrival in Aleppo, there was what passes for an election in Syria. Though running unopposed, President Bashar al-Assad papered the city with an impressive array of campaign posters. Now, the many faces of Assad stare down from every flat surface in sight. Like the model for thespian masks with a hundred variations instead

of the usual two, he is suave in the windows of the posh fashion shops, intense in windows selling Nike sneakers and Adi-
das soccer jerseys, and jolly in windows featuring pint-size
Syrian army uniforms and other children's clothing. On a
few of the posters, he wears an impish grin, which, combined
with his mustache, slightly angular nose, and neatly coiffed
hair, gives him a striking resemblance to a young Walt Disney. On others he looks like the late NASCAR superstar
Dale Earnhardt—particularly on the tricked-out sports cars
wearing presidential silhouettes over their spoilers and racing
stripes. In all his guises he is unavoidable. To the left, Assad.
To the right, Assad. The recently reelected president for life's
face is so ubiquitous I begin to wish his was the head I came
looking for.

I follow the twisting alleys that pass for roads in Aleppo's
old city, and soon not only am I unable to find my way back
to the souk, I have no idea what direction I am walking and
whether I am moving toward familiar territory or away.

Just then a soccer ball bounces into my path. A second
later, a young man jogs through an open doorway a few steps
ahead on the right. He is wearing sneakers and shorts—
unheard of here—and smiles when he sees me. Kicking the
ball into the doorway, he runs back inside without a word.
When I look in after him he says, "Hello, my friend. What
do you hope to find?"

"The mosque," I say.

"Ah. It is easy to get lost here, but this is how to find the
mosque." He walks back through the doorway and points up

a sloping passageway. "Go up this hill until you see the lizard on the wall of the Citadel, then turn right."

"The lizard?" I ask.

"Yes, he climbed up there a few weeks ago and no one dares take him down. Turn there and walk until you see a wall with no lizards at all."

When I reach the top of the hill, I see the Citadel looming above me. Because I am looking for an actual lizard it takes me a moment or two to see the obvious. There, hanging high above the city, is not a lizard but a poster of Assad as big as a drive-in movie screen.

✳

RELICS IN ISLAM are referred to by the Arabic word *athar*, a term that in English relates to the essence or oils of flowers, such as those used to make perfume. The word literally means *trace*, and it refers to the impressions made by Muhammad and other holy ones in the physical world. Most likely, the earliest use of *athar* in the Muslim context referred to the footprints of Muhammad, particularly the footprint that is said to be located at the Dome of the Rock in Jerusalem. It was there, tradition holds, that Muhammad placed his foot on a stone to climb aboard the *Buraq*, the flying beast "larger than a donkey but smaller than a mule" that took the Prophet into the presence of Allah. That last step before this ascent is said to have left a deep imprint in the stone, which since Ottoman times has been preserved under a silver screen. Scholars have suggested that this first instance of Muslim relic veneration was a direct response to the popularity of the Church of the Ascension, just a short walk away, where Jesus's final earthly footprint was a hot spot for Christian pilgrims as early as the fourth century.

It's not surprising that one place of veneration would influence another, despite the fact that they represent two different systems of belief. Islam was born into a world filled with gods: not just Jesus and Yahweh, but the jinn and heroes of ancient Bedouin folk belief. Muhammad and his earliest followers faced the challenge of seeming familiar enough to be comfortable to believers from a variety of religious backgrounds, yet novel enough to attract converts. One element that helped was Islam's ability to incorporate traces of existing traditions into its own.

Combining practices similar to Christian devotion with beliefs held by both Jews and Bedouin tribesmen, Muslims built mosques in honor of biblical and Arab heroes alike.

In all cases, physical displays of memory on the part of other faiths were given the name *athar*, and in being so named they became displays of Muslim memory as well. The word changed the meaning of the objects it came to signify, and it became something new in the process. No longer referring merely to keepsakes of the founder of the faith, or of the many prophets the faith had adopted, it came to indicate any trace of the divine in the world, making every relic a fingerprint left by the creator. As such, like the omnipresent posters of President Assad, relics came to serve as constant reminders of both the divinely ordained power of the followers of Muhammad and the inescapable influence of God.

And yet the power of relics is not precisely like political power; relics in Islam offer hints of greater concerns, realities with rules beyond those that might find it necessary to paper a city with posters. For this reason, *athar* has another meaning as well. It does not refer only to the trace or impression left in rock, or to the trace or impression left in other people's lives. *Athar* refers also to the course of planets as they move through the universe. *Athar* speaks of a celestial trace as much as it does of an emotional or spiritual one. Life and death, presence and absence, this world and all that lies beyond, all bound together in the only form with which we can grapple with such diverse realities: our own.

✳

THERE ARE TWO doors into the *al-Jami al-Kabir*, one for the faithful and one for tourists. As both lead to the same place, the sole purpose of the tourist door seems to be that it routes those with a few extra liras in their pockets past a desk where a small admission charge can be coaxed out of sightseers in the form of a shoe-holding fee.

Having learned my lesson the first time I tried to enter the mosque, I take my shoes off before I pass through the door. Barefooted, I move quickly over the hot stones of the inner courtyard, and, for a moment at least, I seem to pass for a local. I don't realize I have broken another rule by failing to stop and deposit my shoes until a voice rings out behind me.

"Ticket! You must ticket!"

I turn and see two little boys behind a table standing before a worn set of wooden shelves. Dressed in matching red and blue UNICEF soccer jerseys, one of the boys is all business, crouched and ready with a ballpoint pen above a small pad of paper. The other boy stands at his shoulder, a shy apprentice.

"Ten-tee-fife!" the one with the pen says. "We hold for you!"

The shelves behind them, I notice, are made up of several dozen shoe-size cubbies, mostly empty.

"You hold shoes?" I ask.

At the sound of my voice, the boy with the pen nods impatiently. The other boy dissolves into giggles, putting his hands to his face to hide his embarrassment. Only then do I notice that one of his hands isn't a hand at all but a blunt club of flesh, like a fist without fingers. As his giggles subside, he uses the corners of his stump to scratch his ear, staring intently as the other boy manages to keep his composure.

"Yes. Ten-tee-fife, we hold shoes," the boy says.

"Twenty-five?" I dig into my pockets for a coin, but the smallest I can find is marked with two Arabic characters that indicate a fifty-piastre piece. I put it down on the table between us, and the boys exchange perplexed looks at the sight of it. The metal box beside them, I notice, is empty but for an extra pen.

"No change? You can keep," I say. "Keep the coin. Extra for you."

"No! You must ticket!" the seated one says.

"Yes, ticket," I agree. "Fifty, you. Ticket, me."

"No! No! Ten-tee-fife!" He stands up emphatically. "Ten-tee-fife, me. Ten-tee-fife, you. Shoes, me. Ticket, you. Wait!"

With both boys standing I can now see the one in charge is a full head shorter, and it seems a few years younger, than his apparent apprentice. Except for the difference of height, and the fact that only one of them has two good hands, they could be twins.

"Brothers?" I ask.

"Yes, brothers," the smaller one says.

At this, the older one begins giggling again, but the younger one shoves my coin into his brother's hand and speaks to him in Arabic, somehow summoning a commanding tone from his tiny voice. The smaller boy points, and the giggling one takes off in the direction indicated as soon as he understands the instructions he has received. I watch him race across the courtyard, running into a flock of women, their black abayas flapping as he charges through.

The remaining boy studies me for a moment, squinting in the sunlight.

"Where are you?" he asks.

"Where am I *from*? America."

"Ah! America!"

He smiles, waiting for me to respond.

"What is your name?" I ask slowly.

When he only stares in response, I rifle my guidebook to the language section, then try the question in Arabic, "*Maa ismak?*"

"Oh! My name," the boy says in careful English. "My name is Ahmed. My brother, his name is Mahmoud."

Just then Mahmoud returns from his errand. He smacks a twenty-five-piastre coin on the table with his hand, then wipes his brow with the rough end of his other arm, smoothing a few beads of sweat away.

Ahmed slides the coin across the table as if he has just sealed a savvy business deal. "Ten-tee-fife, me, ten-tee-fife you," he says. "Ticket!"

He sits back in his white plastic chair officiously, then presses a pen to his pad, filling in spaces for the number of items, amount paid, shelf occupied. He passes the receipt to me, takes my shoes, and then says, "Okay, Mister. You go now."

Dismissed with a nod, I walk barefoot across the hot stones of the courtyard, then enter the mosque through a door that proves to be directly across from the stairs I stumbled down earlier that day.

A trickle of the faithful come in from the souk, one or two every minute, like water from a leaky pipe. Most move directly toward the center of the mosque, though it seems more than a few have come in seeking only a shortcut out of the marketplace.

The size of the main prayer hall makes every word spoken seem a whisper, yet other sounds echo and fill the space like a flood. The near-constant breathing of vacuum cleaners—a necessity for the upkeep of three acres of carpet, even when all shoes come off at the door—competes with the drone of an elderly imam who sits for hours reciting the Koran in a raspy monotone. From time to time, these sounds are pierced by another: the wailing of infants, sometimes four or five at once. I watch one lying unattended for ten minutes or more, left in the care of the mosque while his mother goes into the souk to do her shopping.

In the center of endless comings and goings from the courtyard to the mosque, from the mosque to the souk, a sign hung from a marble column tells the story of the mosque's unusual history in both English and Arabic.

> In the name of Allah, the most beneficent, the most merciful. Praise be to Allah, Lord of the worlds. May Allah bless our masters, Muhammad, Zakariyya, and all the other prophets and messengers. In Ali bin Shaddad bin Ali's biography, it is mentioned that in 1128 H, in one of the walls of this mosque, there appeared a marble box, closed and sealed with lead, on the box the following is inscribed: "This is one of the organs of Zakariyya the Prophet. This place is an honorable prophetic sign, of which Aleppo is proud."

So I am in the right place. Zacharias is indeed here, or at least once was. But what is this about an "organ"? Is it a mistranslation? I thought I was there to see a head.

A crowd has gathered along the wall beside the entrance to the souk. Men and women, divided by a collapsible wooden partition, stand shoulder to shoulder on either side, pushing forward to reach a brass-colored metal grill, behind which is a window of tinted glass. On the women's side, mothers rub handkerchiefs against the bars and then press them to their children's heads. One mother lifts her baby and holds it to the metal, as high as she can reach, as if she wants any blessing the baby receives this way to be as free of germs as possible. On the men's side, the faithful push forward as one, each reaching out to grip the grill as if it is a ladder to be climbed.

I loiter at the edge of all this for a few minutes before moving toward the wall, not so much pushing my way in as simply getting close enough to the forward movement that I begin to be pulled as if by a current going out to sea. Shoulder to shoulder with the others, I float through the crowd until I stand with my chest pressed against the grill, looking down into a small glass-enclosed space dominated by what seems to be a sarcophagus draped in green cloth. This, I realize, is the tomb of Zacharias. All around me, men pray in Arabic and press their faces against the grill. Some reach through a hole at eye level and drop coins and small photographs into the tomb, believing that the former would be multiplied in thanks for this sacrifice, and that the lives of those depicted in the photographs will be blessed by their new proximity to the holy dead.

Above and surrounding the draped tomb, blue and white tile blinks with the flash of digital cameras, which even the most pious make no hesitation to use. No light comes from the dozen or more hanging oil lamps, placed there to indicate that, despite the bright light and the crowds, this is indeed a place of death.

Before the sarcophagus sits a display case of silver and crystal. Inside, three small orbs of glass seem to hold something within—something brownish in color and organic looking; something with the sad hint of a formerly living thing drained of its life. Behind and around the larger display case, Arabic script presumably explains what is contained therein.

A man beside me reaches into his pocket and produces a passport-size photo, which he slides through an opening in the glass, letting it flutter down away from his hand. When it lands on the silver case and rests there, he presses his fingers against the grill and begins to pray with fervor. Far more than the sarcophagus behind it, whatever is in this case seems to be the object of the greatest devotion and fascination.

Pointing at the spot where his picture had touched down, I ask the man beside me, "Can you read the inscription for me?" He shrugs and points to another man, in a gesture that I presume means this other fellow might help, but from him I receive no reply but a raising of his substantial Syrian eyebrows. As I continue to ask all the men around me, it becomes clear that no one gathered before the grill speaks more than a word or two of English, and my Arabic is, of course, worse than that. There seems to be no way I can find out what I am seeing.

And then I remembered Ahmed. Brief as our conversation was, it seemed he had the best English I've heard in the mosque. Perhaps he could help me make sense of the relics in the case.

Back out in the sunshine of the courtyard, it doesn't take long to find him. He is chasing pigeons, running at them so they swarm toward the foot-washing basins and make the men washing their feet wave their arms to keep them away.

I call out to him. "Ahmed? English? Do you learn English in school?"

His eyes widen at the question. Without answering, he turns and sprints toward me. An instant later, he is by my side. "Hello! English, Mister! English, me, yes!"

Mahmoud comes loping and grinning behind. Before I

have a chance to ask my question, Ahmed shouts at Mahmoud, who jumps at the sound and runs off again. Ahmed keeps calling after him, shouting commands as his brother reaches the desk, grabs a book, and sprints back.

Ahmed snatches it away as soon as Mahmoud returns.

"Look!" Ahmed says, pushing the book into my hands. It is an English instruction book, written in Arabic with the exception of a dozen vocabulary lists in the back. "You, look. I, say: one-two-three-four-five-six-seven-eight-nine-ten . . . very good!"

He flips from one page to the next and points to this list then that before reciting it from memory.

Ahmed flashes a big grin when he is done, and his brother just giggles in admiration. Ahmed shoots him a look of chilling rebuke.

"He no ABCDE," Ahmed says. "He no onetwothreefourfive. Me, onetwothreefourfive, yes! ABCDE, yes!"

At the end of each list, he flashes a grin that shows all his teeth, before declaring, "Me, English, yes!" Then he hooks his thumb at his brother and says gravely, "Him, English, no! You, look. I, say!"

He pushes the book back into my hands, and I flip through the pages until I find a list of body parts.

"Do you know this one?" I ask.

Ahmed's grin disappears as he reads the list. "Hair-head-hand-finger-foot-toe . . . no," he said. Snatching the book back from me, he flips to a friendlier page. "Jannery-Febery-Mars-Appreal-Mayee . . . January-February, me, yes! January-February, him, no!"

I listen to a half dozen recitations of English vocabulary before Ahmed once again shoos me away. As I make my way back toward the relics I see him flip the page to the body parts list and begin to read. When he reaches the end of the page, he repeats the words again silently, closing his eyes and moving his lips as if lost in prayer.

Back inside the mosque, the crowd has thinned in front of the relic window and it seems it is my chance to get a closer look. I still have to determine just what parts of Zacharias I've found.

No sooner have I moved as close as possible to the window than, at the rear of the mosque, a door opens and a handful of pilgrims, men dressed from head to toe in white, enter the prayer hall. A few seconds later, several others follow, each group moving toward the other to undo what seems a momentary separation. Then both sets of doors open again, allowing in a splash of light that precedes and then follows each cluster of pilgrims. They make their way toward the center of the mosque and pile there like a snowdrift, filling a space that seconds before seemed unfillable.

They press in against the grill and quickly engulf me. The tide of pilgrims is so endless and insistent, the imam even looks up for a moment, pausing in his Koranic recital with a finger in his book to hold his place.

They sit cross-legged, mostly in silence, some rocking and praying quietly. Soon the individual prayers give way to a collective humming, and a moment later the humming has transformed itself into a song. It begins as a chorus and then drops out to allow a single voice to rise above the others.

As they sing, I see one of them pause before the English sign. When I am sure he is reading and not merely resting, I slide up beside him and wait for him to finish making his way through the text. He is a tall man, with a long beard the orange-red of a campfire. It has been dyed with henna, a tradition that is said to go back to Muhammad himself. I ask how large a group they are, where they are from, why they have come.

"We are ninety-eight," he says. "We come on pilgrimage from Pakistan."

"To see relics?" I ask. "*Athar*?"

He squints at me. "Yes, to see *athar*. You know this word?"

I tell him I do, but I am not exactly sure what it means.

"It means many things. The tomb of Zacharias, this is *athar*, yes?"

"Yes, but I do not understand why his organs have been placed in that glass case."

"His organs? No, no, he is in the tomb. In the glass case are *athar* of another kind. Very important *athar*: the whiskers of the Prophet Muhammad, peace be upon him. Did you see them? They are orange like mine."

When I look again, I see that indeed the glass orbs do seem to hold hairs. Finally I understand the devotion I am seeing. Zacharias and other borrowed prophets are important to Islam, but there is no one as important as Muhammad, and no relics as important as those that tradition holds were gathered while he was still alive. I scan the crowd of singing pilgrims.

"You come to be close to the Prophet, then?"

"Close? I cannot be close. I come to remind me how far it is I must go. I come to learn how much I have to learn."

As the singing continues around us I ask him about the song. He tells me it is very popular in Pakistan, and in fact it is, in a certain way, about relics, about *athar*. I make a recording of it and later learn its meaning: part poem, part prayer, it is a hymn that speaks of Muhammad as being as far away and yet as present as the moon.

"The moon has returned to us," the pilgrims sing. *"Even when its face is hidden, its trace can be seen."*

The crowd rises as one and again gathers in front of the relic window, getting one last look, one last blessing. As they depart I see a small red and blue blur moving against the current of white-clad travelers. It's Ahmed, still in his soccer jersey, moving toward the window on the relics. Throughout the day, I saw other boys his age run from one side to the other, from men to women and back again as only children are permitted to do. Not Ahmed. He stands patiently behind a cluster of men, and when they step out of the way he takes his turn at the grill. He stands before it for a moment, peering down reverently as he has seen the other men do, but then his age reasserts itself. He grabs hold of the grate and lets his legs go limp, just hanging there, giving the bars his full weight as if on a religious jungle gym.

After a few minutes, he looks to the door and to the walkway that leads to his shoe-checking station. He makes his way back slowly.

"Do you know what is behind the glass?" I ask. "What everyone has come here to see?"

He points to his head.

"*Athar*?" I ask.

He thinks for a minute and seems to summon up some reserve of knowledge he didn't know he had. He is a boy as hungry to learn about my world as I am to learn about his.

"Hair," he says.

WHAT REMAINS

Washington, D.C., where I currently live, is more religious than is usually thought. Across the street from my home—in an area that until recently had the dubious distinction of being the prostitution capital of the nation's capital—there is a convent full of young nuns. They keep to themselves except for their daily outings, when they float single file by my front door in habits as blue as the summer sky. Sometimes, if I happen to be sitting on the stoop when they pass, I can hear entwined with their muted chanting the shouts and fervor of a Pentecostal prayer meeting ringing out from the window of a run-down row house just around the corner. People say Washington is a one-company town, but it is also a city of many gods.

I never noticed too many relics here until I returned from my travels. Now I see them everywhere. It is, after all, a place built not just on swampland but memory, and memory is what first brought relics into the world.

At the moment, however, I am thinking as much about the future as the past. It's a Monday morning and my wife and I set off across town before the sun is up. We drive away from RFK, the dilapidated stadium named for a martyred political saint, away from the old Congressional Cemetery that is now an unlikely dog park, and toward the postcard-perfect section of the city, where the national cult of remembrance is literally carved in stone.

When I look on the great monuments now, so sure and eternal seeming in their white marble certainty, I can only wonder what more mortal forms of memory they are hiding within. We drive down Constitution Avenue until the bright moon of the Capitol Dome rises up before us, glowing like nothing so much, to my travel-weary eyes, as the golden casket of the Buddha's tooth in Kandy.

We drive on, along the National Mall, approaching the Washington Monument, looming like the minaret on the Aleppo mosque; what secret relics might be found in its shadow?

The sky turns pink as we pass the shrines of the war dead, the black mirror of the Vietnam Veterans Memorial always thick with dog tags and flowers, and then the stately white marble of the Lincoln Memorial. Fresh home from my cold visit to Kashmir, it reminds me of the Hazratbal Shrine and the Martyrs' Graveyard of Srinagar.

These aren't just idle comparisons. Most of the places I visited while writing this book are far away—either geographically or religiously, or both. Yet the veneration of relics is not something only other people do. Our national monuments are large-scale reflections of our individual need to remember, not just in spirit but in form. We need to hold on to something to make our memories material. This is why George Washington's hair can be found in collections around the country, as can Abraham Lincoln's blood. According to the Camden County Historical Society in New Jersey, which has one such awful reminder of the sixteenth president's end: "The sheets, pillow cases, blankets, handkerchiefs and other items soaked in Lincoln's blood were cut up and bestowed as honors on members of the cabinet, military officers, high government officials and other Civil War VIPs. These relics were sacred objects." It is said that when Teddy Roosevelt took the oath of office he was wearing a ring containing the great man's hair. As recently as the 1990s, FBI labs were used to authenticate physical relics of George Washington. They are not prayed to, perhaps, but few would doubt that they are some kind of sacred.

We drive on, along the Potomac, a stone's throw from Arlington and the graveyard that is as holy to our national memory as Yad Vashem or the Mount of Olives Cemetery is in Israel. A few miles north and west, we pass under the Gothic spires of Georgetown, the university with the graves of Jesuits at its heart. They are not aboveground as Francis Xavier is in Goa, but they are his brothers. Like him, a new world has grown up around them while they slept.

We pull into a hospital parking lot just as the sun begins to rise. Far from relics here, we are nonetheless aware that this is the kind of place where most everyone we know will die. Inside, as if emerging from a tunnel of memory and what remains of human lives, a child is born.

I have been finishing this book not in the shadow but in the light of that event. The connection my mind makes between a body newly breathing and others so long from their last breath will surely be strange to some. After all, who would want to speak of a newborn child, small and perfect, in the same breath as the abused old bones that populate these pages?

I cannot help but think in the opposite direction, however. How can we begin to consider the meaning of whatever is left of Francis, Joan, Ella, the Buddha, Jesus, Muhammad, or anyone dead but not forgotten, unless we acknowledge, with sadness, with wonder, that they began as small and perfect as the rest of us? These bones—fragile, mortal, beautiful—are where belief begins.

Faith, at least according to Saint Paul's definition, is trust in things unseen. What, then, to make of relics? The point of them is to be seen, meditated upon, keened over. Are they signs of weak faith or strong?

After seeing so many of them for myself, I've come to believe that relics are signs that faith is a lot more complicated than Saint Paul suggests.

Faith is concerned not merely with the unseen, the supernatural, the spiritual. It is not so easily cordoned off as the otherworldly. If faith is not concerned first and foremost with the hard facts of life—with bodies and death and the inevitable end of all that we know—then what does it have to say to us?

Relics seem to me to admit that, yes, while we do have a spiritual dimension to our lives, we are also flesh under the looking glass of all those around us. Our lives and our deaths are witnessed by others, and what our lives might mean to them is mostly beyond our control. We are simultaneously people who need symbols to survive, and we are symbols ourselves. Our bodies—our toes and shins, our foreskins and ribs, our hands and whiskers, our teeth and hair—have the capacity to tell stories we cannot imagine. And the facts of our lives can be as mysterious and in need of explanation as anything that lies beyond.

✳

FROM TIME TO time, now that my traveling is done, I catch myself staring out the kitchen window marveling at the fact that a body in pieces, on display, the object of centuries of devotion, argument, and sometimes ridicule, could have begun as simply human, little different from the helpless and loved creature crying in the next room.

I am thinking of this, of lives transformed into symbols, of symbols so powerful they can transform even death, when I look up and see my wife at my side.

She holds her hand out, palm up, and there between us is

a little scrap of yellowed skin. Brown at the edges, where the blood has dried, it is what's left of an umbilical cord, and it has just fallen off our infant daughter.

"I thought you might want to see it," she says.

She knows me well. And I know her well enough that I do not propose we keep it.

Just a bit of dead skin upon which so much once depended, it goes without ceremony into the trash can.

I have no doubt that relics will always be among us, no matter how spiritually or scientifically advanced we consider ourselves, no matter how quaint or barbaric we find treating "what remains" of those we admire as conduits to something greater than ourselves. For now, though, there are diapers to change and baths to give, lullabies to sing and bills to pay. It's time to put the holy dead behind us, to turn again, as we all must, to the needs of the living.

NOTES

Catch a Martyr by the Toe

This chapter about one of the best-known Jesuits of the past could not have been written without the help of many Jesuits of today. Georgetown University, where I am both a doctoral student in theology and a lecturer in journalism, has an excellent collection of materials on Jesuit history and particularly Saint Francis Xavier, which first allowed me to envision my journey to Goa and then pointed me in the direction of how I might make contact with those who now live beside Xavier's church. Once in India, I was instantly impressed by the hospitality of the members of Goa's

Jesuit community, both those mentioned in the text and those left unnamed. Among the latter, most helpful was Delio Mendonca, SJ, of the Xavier Centre of Historical Research in Goa. Father Delio pointed me toward sources on the history of the Jesuits in India and spoke candidly about the shifting attitudes toward Francis Xavier among Indians, especially concerning the role the saint played in the history of European colonization of the subcontinent.

Several useful books have been written in English, or can be found in English translation, on the life and times of "the Lord of Goa"; among those I consulted were *The Fire of Francis Xavier* by Arthur McCarthy, SJ, and *Saint Francis Xavier* by Jean-Marc Montguerre.

For background on Catholic relic history in general and the phenomenon of incorruptibility in particular, I began with the work of Joan Carroll Cruz. Her two books on the subject, *Relics* and *The Incorruptibles*, are perhaps overly pious in their treatment of the legends and stories of the saints, but they are nonetheless useful both as an example of the devotion relics usually evoke in those who study them and in Cruz's attempt to be comprehensive.

PULLING A LAMA'S LEG

As often as my travels involved extensive preparation and advance scheduling with the subjects involved, I occasionally relied on the happenstance of being in the right place at the right time. I crossed paths with Carmen Straight and the Heart Shrine Relic Tour by accident and quickly learned I'd discovered one of the most interesting—and entrepreneurial—uses of relics today. Carmen was good enough to let me shadow the relic tour for a while in Los Angeles and then to follow as the relics headed out of town.

Back home from the tour, my education in Buddhist relics began with Brian D. Ruppert's *Jewel in the Ashes: Buddha Relics and Power in Early Medieval Japan*. As in many of the stories told in this book, the relationship Ruppert describes between the remains of saints and the attainment and maintenance of political power is complicated and long established. John Strong's *Relics of the Buddha* also provides a great deal of history and was particularly interesting to me, as an occasional memoirist, for its treatment of relics as "extensions of the biographical process." As Strong explains, relics allow those from whom they are taken to continue the story of their lives. In the course of this "extension," they also inevitably become part of the lives of those who venerate them. In this sense, relics might be seen as the stitches that bind the lives of saints and the lives of believers into a common cloth.

This may be especially true for those involved in the relic tour and the Maitreya Buddha Project; the participants I spoke to were devoting their lives to the preservation of relics, and I am grateful to them for taking the time to speak to me about their work.

ONE, TWO, THREE, FORESKIN

Once venerated, then ridiculed, the divine prepuce has become a hard to resist subject of scholarship in recent years. A good place to start is Marc Shell's article "The Holy Foreskin; or, Money, Relics, and Judeo-Christianity" (found in *Jews and Other Differences: The New Jewish Cultural Studies*, edited by Jonathan and Daniel Boyarin), which opened the door for me to consider the place of relics in art history as well is in the history of religion. The foreskin is only briefly mentioned in Patrick Geary's book on the medieval fascination with stolen religious objects (*Furta Sacra: Relic Theft in the Late Middle Ages*), but the book provides such insight into the ideas about the body among the Christian faithful of the time that it is useful well beyond the scope of relics. As in many treatments of the subject, relics for Geary are a key that unlocks nearly every aspect of religion as it was then lived.

They can also occasionally lead to crossing paths with fellow travelers of our own era. As I was working on this chapter I heard of an American travel writer who had gone off to Italy to find the missing prepuce for himself. David Farley's reports from Calcata (published on Slate.com and elsewhere) are both entertaining and informative. At the time of this writing, I do not know if he has found the foreskin but I wish him luck in the pursuit.

A GENTLE RIBBING

I am grateful to Dr. Philippe Charlier not just for spending time with me in Paris but for pointing me in the direction of several books that were indispensable to learning more about the current state of relic investigation. Charlier's own book *Médecin des Morts* is, if my limited French allowed the proper sense of it, an accessible and sometimes humorous elaboration of the practices and implications for using modern medicine to examine ancient bodies. The essays contributed to his yearly colloquy on these issues provided a view of the widening horizon within the field. Another view of relic investigation was provided by Steven Stora's *Treasures from Heaven: Relics from Noah's Ark to the Shroud of Turin*. Like the work of Joan Carroll Cruz, Stora's book is written primarily for people of faith and so it tends to give the benefit of the doubt to relics (particularly the Shroud of Turin) where authenticity is concerned. While I have not been primarily concerned with authenticity, my approach has tended to be the opposite. Nevertheless, I have consistently found that useful information can be discovered in most books about relics regardless of the faith (or lack thereof) of the author.

HANDS ACROSS THE WATER

The story of Elizabeth Romanova has been told in much greater detail than I have attempted here. Christopher Warwick's *Ella: Princess, Saint and Martyr* is the most recent and by far the fullest telling available of her remarkable life. Mother Catherine provided additional pamphlets and clippings during my visit to Jerusalem. She also pointed me toward the most surprising source I encountered during my research. The story of her involvement in the Jericho property dispute, and the brief captivity that resulted, is now a matter of the U.S. Congressional Record. It received significant attention at the time, both in the press and in the halls of Congress, because of the identity of another American-born Orthodox nun. Mother Catherine's companion during her ordeal happened to be the sister of former Clinton administration official George Stephanopoulos, son of a prominent Greek Orthodox family, who no doubt knows a thing or two about relics himself.

THE MOST DANGEROUS WHISKER IN THE WORLD

Shortly before traveling to Kashmir to see the disputed Hazratbal hair, I was lucky enough to take part in Professor Ariel Glucklich's Georgetown University graduate seminar on the concept of dharma in Hinduism. Reading primary texts of Vedic literature as well as the cultural anthropology of Mary Douglas and others, I came to see how the idea of dharma as the all-purpose ordering principle of the universe can lead to questions of "Hinduness" related to this most Muslim of Indian states. For background on Kashmir, I found most helpful several books I picked up in the excellent bookshops of Srinagar. Among them, Andrew Whitehead's *A Mission in Kashmir*; Sumantra Bose's *Kashmir: Roots of Conflict, Paths to Peace*; and finally (and of course) Salman Rushdie's great short story about the Hazratbal relic, "The Prophet's Hair."

My way into Kashmir was made smooth by the kindness of the New York–based Kashmiri journalist Basharat Peer, who from afar introduced me to Hilal Bhat and Javeed Shah. Hilal and Javeed acted as my hosts and guides while I was in Srinagar and became my new friends as a result. Hilal's family south of the city was kind enough to invite me to celebrate Eid with them, which remains my warmest memory from many months of traveling.

TOOTH AND NAIL

If not for this book, I surely would have lived all my days without visiting Sri Lanka, and it would have been a great loss. My time in Kandy was unfortunately brief and so I was forced to do much of my research on the meaning of the tooth relic after the fact. Toward this end, two sources helped most of all: *Embodying the Dharma: Buddhist Relic Veneration in Asia*, edited by David Germano and Kevin Trainor; and Stephen C. Berkwitz's *The History of the Buddha's Relic Shrine*, a translation of the original Sinhalese recounting of the history of Buddhism in Sri Lanka that details how the tooth temple came to be the focus of so much spiritual and political power.

SPLITTING HAIRS

Shortly after returning from Syria, I dropped in at the Annapolis, Maryland, office of Professor Brannon Wheeler, a religious historian who teaches at the U.S. Naval Academy. I had brought his book *Mecca and Eden: Ritual, Relics, and Territory in Islam* with me on my travels to provide some historical context for the Islamic sites I was seeing. Most of the primary texts cited in the chapter come from Wheeler, whose facility with the necessary languages and talent for fitting ancient practices with modern relevance (he has also published peer-reviewed articles on surfing as ritual) combine to produce uncommonly readable scholarship.

As helpful as his book was, however, he provided perhaps the insight most useful to this book during a brief conversation. Sitting in his Naval Academy office with midshipmen hurrying across the quad below, Professor Wheeler mentioned the work other scholars had done that purported to prove that the faithful venerate relics because to stand before the remains of a religious figure is to feel the continued "presence" of that saint. "I disagree," he told me, "because I don't think people who venerate relics are stupid. They know what it means to be dead and gone; they may be thinking of Muhammad when they see his whiskers, but they don't mistake memory or imagination for *presence*. They know they are experiencing *absence* first of all."

For expressing this thought so plainly and powerfully, I am grateful to Professor Wheeler. For showing me the truth of it, I cannot thank enough the hundreds of believers of all kinds, from all over the world, who talked to me about faith during my research for this book. Together they have shown me that people who involve relics in their religious lives may do something strange and mysterious, but they do not do it blindly.

PETER MANSEAU is the author of the memoir *Vows* and the novel *Songs for the Butcher's Daughter*. He is also the coauthor (with Jeff Sharlet) of *Killing the Buddha: A Heretic's Bible*. He lives with his wife and two daughters in Washington, D.C., where he teaches writing and studies religion at Georgetown University.